A Cambridge Keepsake

Photography: Andrew Pearce   *Fotogenix Publishing*   Text: Debi Pearce

First published in Great Britain 2005
by Fotogenix Publishing
Telephone: 01767 677086
www.fotogenix.co.uk

Printed by Bath Press Ltd, Bath, UK
Photography © and editing: Andrew Pearce ARPS
Text © and design: Debi Pearce
Map design © Louise Evans

ISBN 0-9547355-1-X

A Cambridge Keepsake

Photography: Andrew Pearce   *Fotogenix Publishing*   Text: Debi Pearce

First published in Great Britain 2005
by Fotogenix Publishing
Telephone: 01767 677086
www.fotogenix.co.uk

Printed by Bath Press Ltd, Bath, UK
Photography © and editing: Andrew Pearce ARPS
Text © and design: Debi Pearce
Map design © Louise Evans

ISBN 0-9547355-1-X

Select photographs reproduced by kind permission of
the Masters, Principals, Presidents, Provosts, Fellows and Scholars of the following Colleges:
Peterhouse, Clare, Corpus Christi, Gonville and Caius, King's, Queens', Jesus, Christ's, St. John's,
Trinity, Trinity Hall, Emmanuel, Magdalene, Downing, Sidney Sussex, Pembroke, St. Catharine's.

CONTENTS

Overleaf: St. John's College from the Backs
Title Page: Spring view of King's College Chapel

INTRODUCTION

Cambridge is famous above all for its illustrious University, but its tale begins long before the arrival of the first academic refugees from riotous Oxford in 1209. There is evidence of settlement here in neolithic times, and geography has served it well. Its combination of a hill, overlooking a river negotiable by seafaring ships, all at an intersection of important trade routes, proved irresistible to Roman, Danish and Norman invaders. So it was that a thriving market town evolved, based around the river Cam. The city coat of arms still displays sea horses and ships in acknowledgement of its sea trading history. Today the population of Cambridge is over 100,000, with three million visitors each year.

As the University began to flourish, the contrast between the dirty, difficult living conditions of the ordinary townspeople and the privileged, beautiful environment of the colleges became a source of conflict. The 'King's Ditch', Cambridge's defensive boundary, was an open sewer that posed a threat as great as any invading force. By 1574 this menace of disease compelled Town and Gown to collaborate, creating Hobson's Conduit which brought cleaner drinking water to the town. How many academic advancements at Cambridge have occurred partly because of the Black Death: plague carried by fleas on the black rat? Several colleges were founded to replace learned men lost to this disease. Without its deadly influence, Stephen Hawking and Francis Crick, of Gonville and Caius, might never have developed theories on time and space or discovered the structure of DNA. Big Ben's Westminster may have rung another tune if its composer, Trinity Hall's William Crotch and his teacher Dr. Jowett, had studied elsewhere.

Bicycles crowd the Cambridge streets: the 15,000 students who attend the 31 colleges comprising the University are not allowed to own cars. The obvious reasons of parking and congestion are true today, but in the early 1900s, college authorities were more concerned about the 'romantic' potential for undergraduates that a vehicle offered!

Left: A Scots Piper ascends Castle Mound.

Malting Lane

Not until 1788 did Cambridge pave its first street, in Petty Cury, or introduce street lighting. Between 1575 and 1670, householders who could afford it were required to hang out a light for three hours after 6pm between 1st November and 2nd February, except on moonlit nights. It was a hazardous place, too; undergraduates were forbidden to carry lighted torches because of the 'great terror and apprehension' it caused. Some original gas lamps (above) are still in use today.

Cambridge has been a major arena of political conflict. It has seen changes of monarchy, Henry VIII's divorces and dissolution of the monasteries, followed by his daughter Mary Tudor's religious purging. The peaceful green space of Midsummer Common was once the place where 'heretics' were burned at the stake, and criminals were whipped in the market-place. Oliver Cromwell found many Royalist adversaries here during the Civil War, and his henchman, the infamous William Dowsing, was sent to destroy all he could find of the colleges' Catholic paraphernalia. Intermingled with these power struggles was the riotous uprising of townspeople. Today a lamp-post in the centre of Parker's Piece is known as the 'Reality Checkpoint': a dividing line between two very different worlds! But the massive gates of the colleges, once intended to keep common people at bay, now open regularly to visitors. The relationship between Town and Gown is a symbiotic one. Income of rents from Cambridge businesses assists the University in the costly upkeep of its beautiful buildings, while local trade depends heavily on tourists attracted by the colleges and their fascinating history.

Cambridge is growing more attractive as stonework stained by years of chimney smoke and car exhaust is gradually cleaned. The quiet that allowed Isaac Newton to deduce the outcome of a sea battle between the English and Dutch from the sounds of cannon fire retreating towards our shores can never be recreated, but restriction of traffic from the central areas has created a more tranquil setting in which to appreciate this ancient and unique city.

Opposite: Ancient buildings in Bridge Street

THE UNIVERSITY

Cambridge University began around 800 years ago, when scholars fled from troubles in Oxford. There must, however, have been some educational establishment here already to attract them. It is speculated that the School of Pythagoras, today hidden within the grounds of St. John's, was Cambridge's first centre of learning. Here it is said that monks from Crowland Abbey would preach the Christian faith alongside academic subjects. Scholars began aged around fourteen, with only a little knowledge of Latin, and their first task was to learn the language, before embarking on a threefold course called the *trivium*, covering Grammar, Logic and Rhetoric. Then came the *quadrivium* of arithmetic, geometry, music and astronomy, qualifying the student to become a lecturer himself as a Master of Arts. Examinations were originally oral, and today's examination term *'Tripos'*, stems from the three-legged stool that was sat on during these disputations.

Gowns vary according to college, degree and status. Students today have a wide range of subject options, usually studying for three or four years before their final, written exams, but the sense of achievement can be no less now than 700 years ago.

Left: The Bedell carries a silver mace given by the Duke of Buckingham in 1626.

Right: Senate House, built in 1722, is the venue for the University Congregations. The majority of these take place in June, when this usually refined and stately landmark becomes a colourful mass of happy graduates and their proud families. This is the only time that the immaculate lawn may be walked upon.

The huge Warwick Vase was presented by the Duke of Northumberland in 1842. It is a replica of an original marble vase, found at the bottom of Lake Tivoli near Hadrian's Roman villa. This is now displayed at the Burrell Collection in Glasgow.

Written examinations were introduced around 1772, and the range of subjects gradually grew to incorporate Law and Medicine. However, confirmed religion remained a pre-requisite for a degree until 1871. Fellows (members of a college usually elected for teaching, research or as a subject specialist), had further restrictions: until 1881 they could not marry unless they gave up their fellowship. Shortly after this came the introduction of the first colleges for women at Newnham and Girton, but they were not admitted to official degrees until 1947. It would be another 25 or so years before the other colleges accepted female students for the first time, with Magdalene the last to do so in 1988. When students today matriculate (enrol with a college), they are assigned to a tutor who oversees their academic progress and general welfare. Discipline is enforced by the Proctor, supported by the 'bulldogs', who traditionally patrolled the colleges in pairs: one chosen as a sprinter, the other for stamina in the chase. In extreme cases a student may be 'sent down' i.e. expelled. In the past, such a departing undergraduate would be escorted to the station by a mock funeral procession! The students pass daily under the watchful eyes of the college Porters, who are no mere luggage-bearers. As official gate-keepers they have an impressive knowledge of the staff and students. At the cutting edge of intellectual advancement the workload is demanding, but the noticeboards by the Porters' lodges hint at the exciting variety of pursuits that enrich the life of a Cambridge student.

Left: 'Graduands' set off from their college to Senate House to receive their degrees. Only after the pronunciation of their admission in Latin by the Vice- Chancellor are they fully- fledged 'graduates'. Degree days for undergraduates are a familiar sight in June, but ceremonies relating to higher degrees may take place throughout the year.

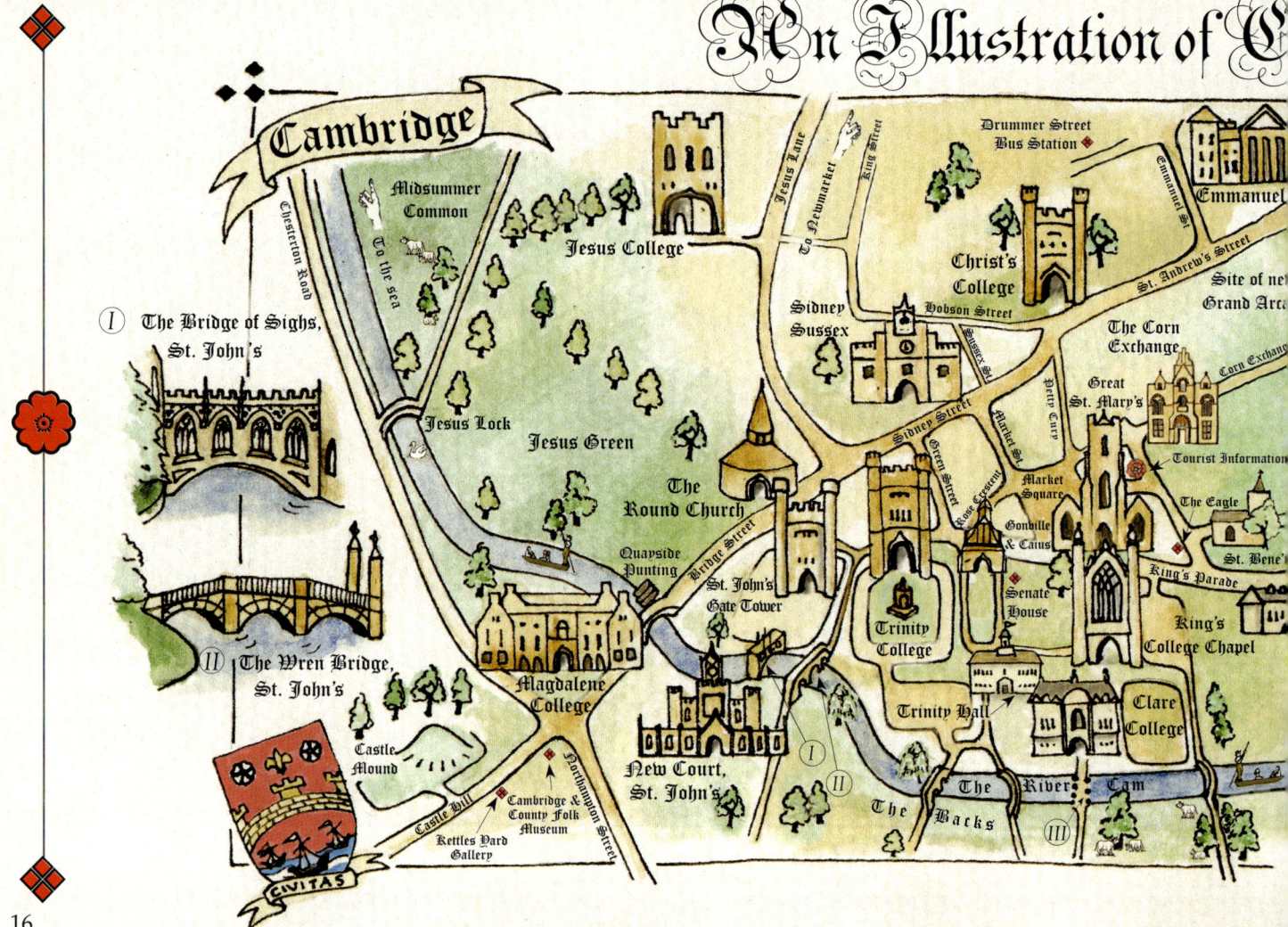

Cambridge

Midsummer Common

Jesus College

Drummer Street
Bus Station

Emmanuel

Christ's College

Site of new
Grand Arc

Jesus Lane

To Newmarket

King's Street

Jesus Lock

Chesterton Road

To the sea

I The Bridge of Sighs,
St. John's

Sidney
Sussex

Hobson Street

St. Andrew's Street

The Corn
Exchange

Corn Exchange

Jesus Green

Great
St. Mary's

Sidney Street

Sussex St.

Market St.

Petty Cury

The Round Church

Quayside
Punting

Bridge Street

St. John's
Gate Tower

Tourist Information

The Eagle

Market
Square

Green Street

Rose Crescent

Gonville
& Caius

St. Bene'

King's Parade

King's
College Chapel

II The Wren Bridge,
St. John's

Magdalene
College

Trinity
College

Senate
House

Castle
Mound

New Court,
St. John's

Trinity Hall

I

II

Clare
College

Castle Hill

Cambridge &
County Folk
Museum

Northampton Street

Kettles Yard
Gallery

The Backs

The River Cam

III

CIVITAS

16

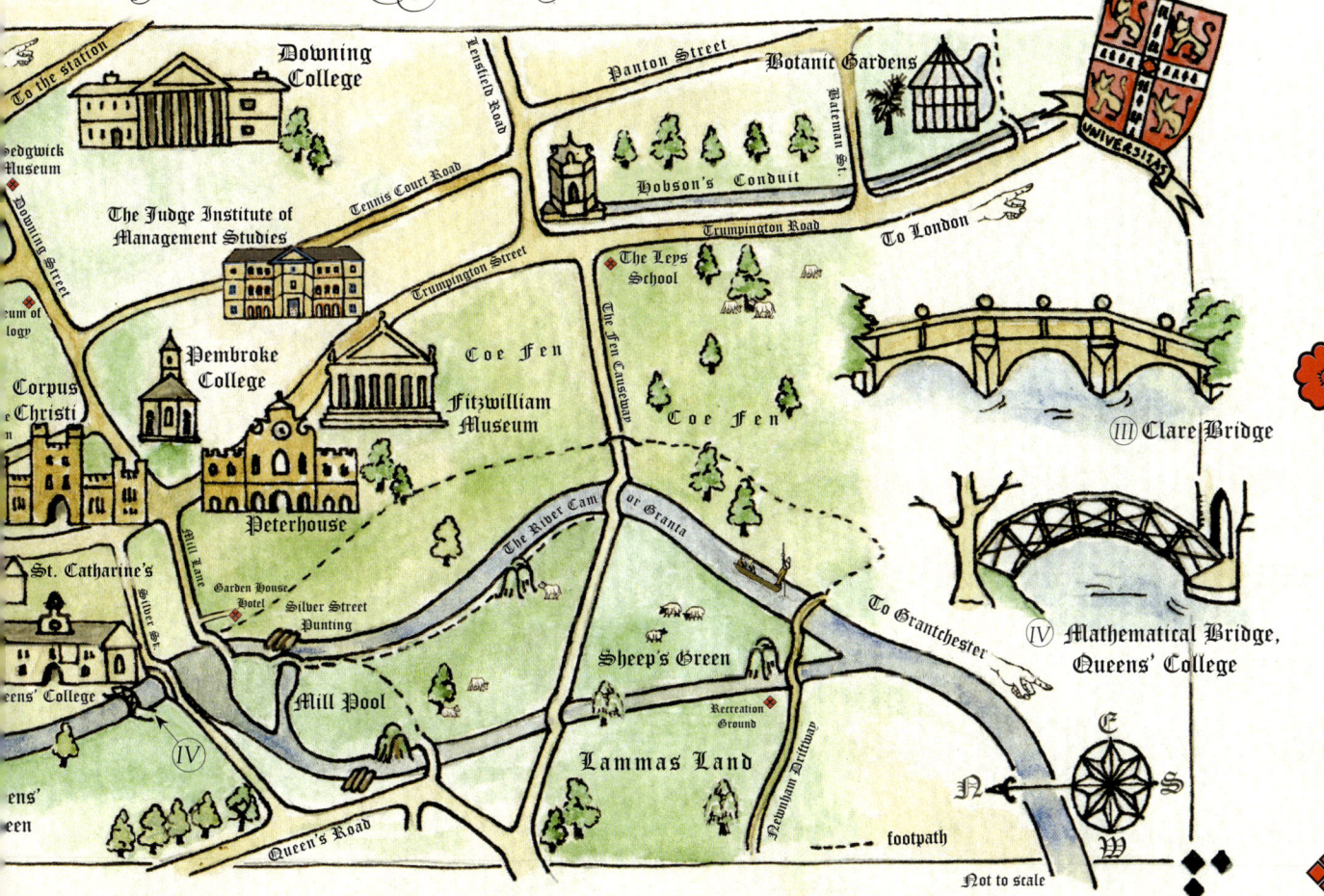

nbridge and its Colleges

To the station

Downing College

Sedgwick Museum

Downing Street

Museum of ... logy

The Judge Institute of Management Studies

Lensfield Road

Tennis Court Road

Panton Street

Botanic Gardens

Bateman St.

Hobson's Conduit

Trumpington Road

To London

UNIVERSITAS

Corpus e Christi n

Pembroke College

Trumpington Street

Coe Fen

The Leys School

The Fen Causeway

Coe Fen

III Clare Bridge

Fitzwilliam Museum

Peterhouse

St. Catharine's

Mill Lane

Silver St.

Garden House Hotel

Silver Street Punting

The River Cam

or Granta

To Grantchester

IV Mathematical Bridge, Queens' College

eens' College

eens' een

IV

Mill Pool

Sheep's Green

Recreation Ground

Queen's Road

Lammas Land

Newnham Driftway

footpath

Not to scale

N E S W

17

KING'S

King's College Chapel must be Cambridge's definitive structure. It dominates the town and the Backs, and one can only wonder how much more magnificent King Henry VI's college would have been if his full plans had been implemented. He laid the chapel foundation stone on 25th July, St. James' Day, in 1446. The original title of his college was 'The King's College of our Lady and St. Nicholas'. The first Rector and 70 scholars hardly required such an enormous place of worship. But Henry was an intensely devout Christian, and achieved unofficial sainthood following his execution. This wonderful building could be seen as his personal tribute to the glory of God.

Altogether five kings contributed funding to the chapel over 90 years, with Henry VIII seeing its completion in 1536. His predecessor had stipulated a building '... *in large fourme clene and substancial, settyng a parte superfluite of too gret curious werkes of entaille and besy moldyng*', but the interior detail is staggering nonetheless. A visiting child might be convinced of the college's name by counting the number of crowns in the antechapel. These were added by Henry VII along with the beautiful stone Tudor insignia of roses, greyhounds, dragons and portcullises. To then see the carved wooden organ screen and choir stalls, to admire Rubens' *Adoration of the Magi* behind the altar, and to take in the fabulous detail of the stained glass windows and fan vaulted ceiling, is almost too much for a single visit.

Left: In spring this view of King's College Chapel is enhanced by a carpet of crocus which matches the College colours.

King's Chapel is famous for its music: in 1791 Joseph Haydn admired the chapel ceiling. Saint Saëns complimented the 'admirable choristers', and Yehudi Menuhin performed a charity concert here in 1965. Each Christmas since 1928 King's Festival of Nine Lessons and Carols has been broadcast worldwide.

*Right: The Fellows'
Building was James
Gibbs' last work in
Cambridge, and is named
after him. This imposing,
symmetrical structure,
built with Portland stone,
holds its own status
next to the chapel. Its
foundation stone, laid
in 1724, is a partially
cut stone abandoned by
builders working on the
chapel when they heard of
Henry VI's capture.*

*Preceding Page:
Early morning mist in
Bodley's Court*

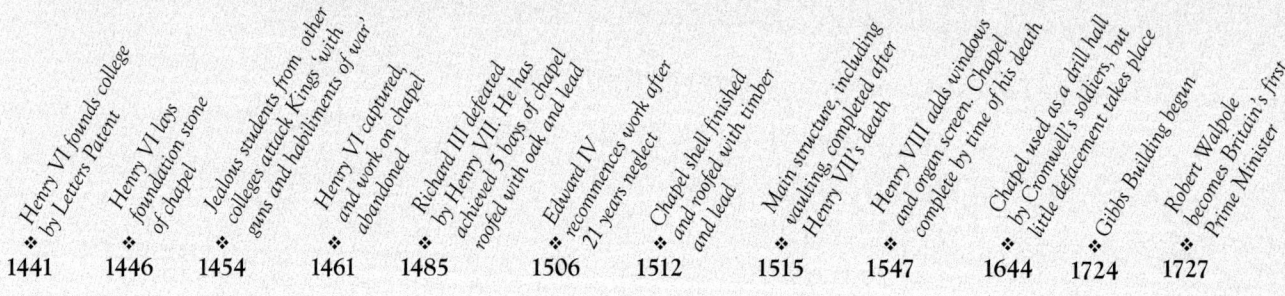

Henry VI founds college by Letters Patent
❖
1441

Henry VI lays foundation stone of chapel
❖
1446

Jealous students from other colleges attack Kings' 'with guns and habiliments of war'
1454

Henry VI captured, and work on chapel abandoned
❖
1461

Richard III defeated by Henry VII. He has achieved 5 bays of chapel roofed with oak and lead
1485

Edward IV recommences work after 21 years neglect
1506

Chapel shell finished and roofed with timber and lead
❖
1512

Main structure, including vaulting, completed after Henry VII's death
1515

Henry VIII adds windows and organ screen. Chapel complete by time of his death
❖
1547

Chapel used as a drill hall by Cromwell's soldiers, but little defacement takes place
1644

Gibbs Building begun
❖
1724

Robert Walpole becomes Britain's first Prime Minister
❖
1727

22

The election of a Provost can be a lengthy procedure if a stalemate in the voting arises, as it did in January 1742. The fellows were obliged to remain in the extremely chilly chapel, where the debate took place, until an agreement had been reached. This took three days and nights! Dr. Daniel Wray recounts:

'A friend of mine, a curious man, tells me, he took a survey of his brothers at the hour of two in the morning ... Some wrapped in blankets, erect in their stalls like mummies; others, asleep on cushions, like so many Gothic tombs. Here a red cap over a wig; there a face lost in the cape of a rug. One blowing a chafing dish with a surplice sleeve; another warming a little negus, or sipping Coke upon Littleton, i.e. tent and brandy. Thus did they combat the cold of that frosty night; which has not killed any one of them, to my infinite surprize'.

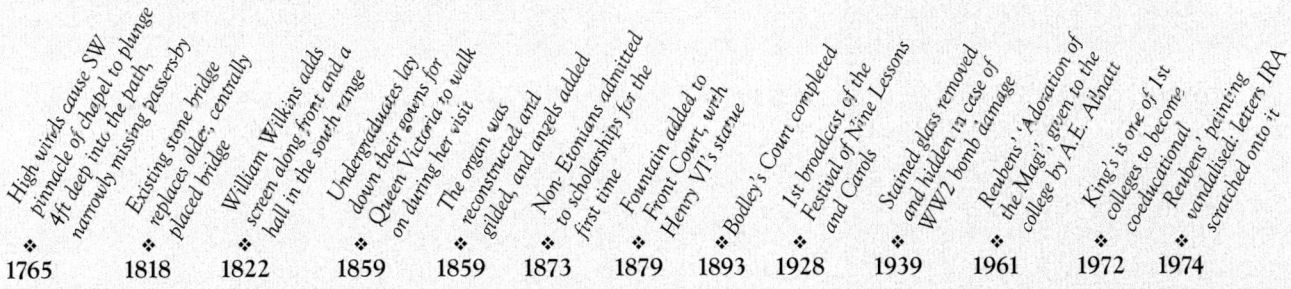

High winds cause SW pinnacle of chapel to plunge 4ft deep into the path, narrowly missing passers-by
1765

Existing stone bridge replaces older, centrally placed bridge
1818

William Wilkins adds screen along front and a hall in the south range
1822

Undergraduates lay down their gowns for Queen Victoria to walk on during her visit
1859

The organ was reconstructed and gilded, and angels added
1859

Non-Etonians admitted to scholarships for the first time
1873

Fountain added to Front Court, with Henry VI's statue
1879

Bodley's Court completed
1893

1st broadcast of the Festival of Nine Lessons and Carols
1928

Stained glass removed and hidden in case of WW2 bomb damage
1939

Reubens' 'Adoration of the Magi', given to the college by A.E. Allnatt
1961

King's is one of 1st colleges to become coeducational
1972

Reubens' painting vandalised: letters IRA scratched onto it
1974

Originally, King's scholars all came from Henry VI's other educational foundation, Eton, and they were resented by the other colleges to the point of violence because of their privileges. Until 1851, King's students could claim a degree without taking an examination, and were not bound by the authority of the University Proctors. Non-Etonians were first admitted to scholarships in 1873. King's was one of the first colleges to become co-educational and took the lead in making gown-wearing optional.

The chapel architecture has always tempted adventurous climbers. A coin dated 1760 was once found 20 feet below the summit of a pinnacle. In 1932 two umbrellas appeared attached to the spires, one of which was shot down by a volunteer student. A Union Flag replaced it shortly afterwards, but this time the patriotic sharp-shooter felt unable to fire upon his own flag, so steeplejacks had to be sent up. Some rooftop visitors are legitimate, however: eminent guests are invited to have their footprint etched into the lead of the chapel roof.

Left and above: Bodley's Court

The King's College of the early years may have had an indolent reputation, but today its list of eminent scholars is impressive. It includes Britain's first Prime Minister Robert Walpole, and journalist and politician Martin Bell. The poet Rupert Brooke also studied here. He evokes his experience of being a King's student in a candid poem, taken from his letter to A.F. Scholfield in 1913:

My heart is sick for several things
Only to be found in King's ...

I do recall those haunts with tears,
The Backs, the Chapel, and the Rears ...

O Places of perpetual mire,
Localities of my desire,
O lovely, O remembered gloom
And froust of Chetwynd lecture room ...
O spots my memory is gilding,
O Jumbo Arch! O Wilkins Building! ...

Haunts where I drank the whole damn night!
Place where I catted till the light!
Dear spot where I was taken short,
O Bodley's Court! O Bodley's Court!

Right: Not all King's 'high-flying' members
are human! House martins nest each year in the
ornamental ceiling of the Great Gate.
Overleaf: King's Chapel from the Backs

Queens' Mathematical Bridge

QUEENS'

Why should kings get all the glory? Margaret of Anjou, young wife of Henry VI, saw no reason at all. His own ambitious college project made her 'restless with holy emulation of her husband's bounty'. She chose an existing college: St. Bernard's, founded by Andrew Doket in 1446, and refounded it as 'The Queen's College of St. Margaret and St. Bernard' in 1448 'to laud and honneure of sexe feminine'. Her dear friend Elizabeth Woodville later became Queen herself as wife of Edward IV, and issued new statutes for the college in 1475. Royal patronage continues today with our own Queen Elizabeth II.

Queens' played a significant part during the Renaissance in the 1500s as a centre of the new humanist and Protestant philosophies. Greek was introduced alongside traditional Latin, and the status of classical literature and rhetoric rose in the university curriculum. Wise John Fisher presided here. While Fisher did not concur with the 'new learning' of Protestantism the arrival of his friend, the Dutch scholar Erasmus, with his incisive intellect and knowledge of Greek, was a great asset. Erasmus found Cambridge uncomfortably like his marshy homeland and complained much, especially about the 'raw, smal and windy' beer. Queens' President Isaac Milner commented in 1814,

> 'We have no relic of him except a huge corkscrew
> ..and I am afraid there was nothing in his principles
> to keep him from making very assiduous use of it'.

Queens' combined sundial and moondial was created in 1642 and restored in 1968. It is designed to show more than time of day, (read by the position of the gnomon's shadow over the Roman numerals). The dual symbols show the zodiac signs with their associated planetary object, (only seven were known then). Reading the shadow of the ball on the gnomon between the green lines gives the zodiac phase of the year. It also shows the compass bearing of the sun, its elevation above the Horizon, and the month. However, inaccuracies in restoration and shifting variables in the Earth's orbit can make this unreliable.

Overleaf: Cloister Court

Queens' remained staunchly Royalist during the Civil War, when they joined forces with St. John's and Jesus to send 2065 ounces of silver to aid the king. Cromwell punished them by destroying their bridge, and Dowsing records on December 26 1643,

> 'We beat down about 110 Superstitious Pictures besides Cherubims and Ingravings, where none of the Fellows would put on their Hatts in all the time they were in Chapell and we digged up the Steps for 3 hours and brake down 10 or 12 Apostles and Saints within the Hall'.

Cambridge's only surviving wooden bridge, the 'Mathematical Bridge' is a charming feature of the college. Today's bridge is a reconstruction of the 1749 original. Popular myth attributes its intricate structure to Newton, but it was built after his death in 1727: William Etheridge was the designer and James Essex the builder.

Queens' is approached from the town via narrow Silver Street. This was a hazardous business in the time of scholar John Lloyd who once threw a chair out of the window at a passing carriage. He beat up the unfortunate servant sent to investigate, and threw him into the mud by the river. When the driver himself arrived the same fate awaited him. Lloyd's punishment by the college was to formally apologise and to memorise a Cicero oration!

Overleaf: The Mathematical Bridge

Andrew Dokett founds St. Bernard's College	College refounded by Queen Margaret	Riverside buildings erected	Queen Elizabeth Woodville becomes patroness	Cloisters built, forming Cloister Court	Erasmus visits college	Long Gallery created	Walnut Tree Building completed	Wooden Bridge erected	Apostrophe in Queen's moved to Queens'	New Chapel by G.F. Bodley completed	1st telephones installed	Wooden beams of cloisters by President's Lodge uncovered	Elizabeth Bowes-Lyon, (Queen Mother), becomes patroness	Erasmus Building by Basil Spence erected	Cripps Court begun	Admission of women
1446	1448	1460	1465	1495	1510	1595	1618	1749	1831	1891	1907	1923	1949	1959	1970	1980

SOUVENT · ME · SOUVIENT

CHRIST'S

Christ's College was the creation of Lady Margaret Beaufort. In 1505 she chose to refound an existing institution: God's House, founded by William Bingham in 1439 as a college to train schoolmasters in grammar. Continuity was ensured by keeping its last Master on as the first Master of Christ's. The society enlarged considerably to comprise a Master, 12 fellows and up to 47 scholars: only King's was larger at this time.

Lady Margaret, mother of Henry VII, was a learned and charitable woman who gave benefactions for many purposes throughout her life. Christ's was her first college, undertaken, like St. John's six years later, with the advice of John Fisher. She took a keen interest in her project and a compassionate view of her scholars. At this time miscreants under 21 were punished by whipping. It is recorded that one day while visiting the college, she chanced to look out of the window and 'saw the dean call a faulty scholar to correction; to whom she said *'Lenté, lenté!'* 'Gently, gently!' as accounting it better to mitigate his punishment than to procure his pardon'. Good conduct was a priority, however. The first statutes banned students from many activities including drinking parties, carrying weapons, and keeping hawks or dogs. Dice or card games were also forbidden except in the hall at Christmas. Clean surplices were required to be worn in chapel, and if any college member 'do wipe his hande or fingers of the table clothe, he shall pay for every time 1d'.

The heraldic ornamentation is especially well maintained at Christ's, and has much in common with St. John's. The motto 'Souvent me souvient' (I remember often) is seen at both colleges. The mythical antelope-like Yales and the Portcullis represent the Beaufort family. The daisies (marguerites) are a play on the foundress' name, Margaret. The Rose was the emblem of Henry VII and the Greyhound is associated with the Tudor dynasty. Expenditure on decoration was considerable. Outlay for painting of woodwork and images in 1510 refers to:
'Item to Paule Smyth for certen coloures as in white led red led generall mastyke vernysch yelowe moty orpment roch vemylyon vergres Bisse oyle coperose white vitriall wex Cereuse Synoper red oker yelowe oker Inde ffyne gold iiij C di'.

Left: First Court, with Lady Margaret's elaborate coat of arms

1439	❖	Bingham founds God's House
1505	❖	Lady Margaret refounds it as Christ's College
1509	❖	Evidence of earliest English wallpaper, discovered during 1900s refurbishment, dates from this time
1609	❖	King James instigates planting of mulberry trees to feed silk worms
1625	❖	Milton enters college
1640	❖	Fellows' Building completed
1714	❖	Street front refaced
1769	❖	Refacing of interior court by James Essex completed
1825	❖	Range built on south side of second court
1827	❖	Darwin enters college
1875	❖	Hall rebuilt by Gilbert Scott
1897	❖	Old Library extended by G.F. Bodley
1899	❖	Chapel restored by Bodley
1911	❖	Reconstruction of the Lodge, funded by Sir Arthur Shipley
1969	❖	New Court built by Sir Denys Lasdun

Left: Christ's beautiful gardens contain stately trees set amongst the floral displays skilfully designed to give colour almost all year round.

Christ's location at the end of St. Andrew's Street placed it close to the infamously filthy King's Ditch, originally dug as a defence for the town. This was a contributing factor to the 'visitations' of plague that periodically beset Cambridge. The devastating effects on Christ's College are clear in Mr. Mead's letter dated April 24th, 1630,

> 'Our University is in a manner wholy dissolved: all meetings & Exersises ceasing. In many Colledges almost none left ... We have taken all our Officers into the Colledge & none must stirre out. If he doth he is to come in no more. ... Thus we live as close Prisoners, & I hope without danger'.

By the 1700s, the college's original red brick and clunch construction was in need of repair, and James Essex was commissioned to reface many of the buildings between 1758 and 1770. The college has steered a fairly moderate course through the extremes of political and religious change, and produced many reflective, sensitive individuals. The poet Calverley's pranks livened up the atmosphere in the 1850s. Wordsworth, in his autobiographical poem, *The Prelude*, recalls a visit to the rooms where poet John Milton allegedly lodged as a student.

> '... One of a festive circle, I poured out
> Libations, to thy memory drank, till pride
> And gratitude grew dizzy in a brain
> Never excited by the fumes of wine
> Before that hour, or since'.

Mathematics and science have also flourished here. Charles Darwin entered Christ's intending to qualify as a clergyman. Ironically his fascination with insects, acquired while studying here, would ultimately lead him into conflict with the church when he wrote his theory of evolution in *The Origin of Species*.

Above: Milton's Mulberry. No college garden in Cambridge could be a more inspiring refuge for a poet. It is unlikely that Milton planted the mulberry tree named after him, but he may have spent time in its shade, if that was allowed! His fellow scholars taunted him as 'The Lady of Christ's' for his delicate appearance, but the tree has been venerated: turf has been banked around it to preserve it.

ST. JOHN'S

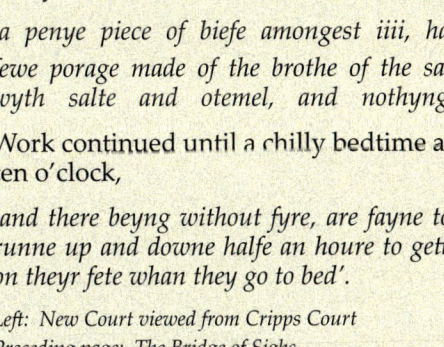

Lady Margaret Beaufort found herself in a position of having more money than time left to spend it. She had already founded Christ's College and was considering a bequest to Westminster Abbey. Her wise counsellor John Fisher advised her to bestow it instead on the monastic Hospital of St. John, which had already featured in Bishop Balsham's first, unsuccessful attempt to create an academic institution. Lady Margaret died in 1509, leaving her will, which was unproved till 1512. Fisher obtained a charter two years later but the college did not open until 1516.

The college rose to high academic status in its early years, but life was tough. Scholars slept and studied in a room shared with their tutor, tucking their small beds under his during the day. They would rise between four and five a.m, pray in chapel for an hour and study until dinner at ten, which consisted of,

'a penye piece of biefe amongest iiii, havynge a fewe porage made of the brothe of the same biefe, wyth salte and otemel, and nothynge elles.'

Work continued until a chilly bedtime at nine or ten o'clock,

'and there beyng without fyre, are fayne to walk or runne up and downe halfe an houre to gette a heate on theyr fete whan they go to bed'.

Left: New Court viewed from Cripps Court
Preceding page: The Bridge of Sighs

41

St. John's extensive series of courts has evolved creating an almost illusory, maze-like effect. Second Court was an ill-fated project. Benefactor Lady Shrewsbury proved unable to foot the entire bill of £3665, architect Ralph Symonds lost a hand during its construction, and his colleague Gilbert Wigge was sued by the college and imprisoned. St. John's was one of the first colleges to extend across the river. It has two bridges. The handsome stone bridge, attributed to Sir Christopher Wren, replaced an earlier wooden structure. It was built by Robert Grumbold, son of Thomas Grumbold who built the bridge at Clare . The enclosed Bridge of Sighs, much admired by Queen Victoria, had the added advantage of making nocturnal escapades difficult for students.

Elaborate New Court, with its 'Wedding Cake' tower, has a blank clock face offering great potential for student pranks. A bold individual once climbed up and painted one on. The Master noticed it next morning and informed a porter that the clock had stopped. Only when a man was sent up to investigate did the lack of a working mechanism became apparent.

The existing college chapel was built in 1869, and its elegant square tower is a key feature of the Cambridge skyline. Since 1902 it has been a tradition for the choir to sing Palestrina's *'O Rex Gloriae'* from its roof on Ascension Day. Not everyone uses the stairs, however! The Cambridge Nightclimbers once dressed a statue on the outside of the chapel in a surplice. No ladder would reach, so a rather stout porter kindly volunteered to be lowered on a rope from a higher window to remove them. All went well until it was discovered that he was too heavy to pull back up. The unfortunate gentleman was stranded, swaying gently in the breeze, until a longer rope could be found to lower him to safety.

Overleaf: Dusted with snow, New Court's neo-Gothic 'Wedding Cake' tower truly lives up to its name.

Opposite: Lady Margaret's statue looks down benevolently from above the entrance to St. John's. The design resembles Christ's, with its founder's mythical 'yales', and the daisies, or marguerites that symbolise her name.

Left: St. John's beautiful Chapel contains the plaster model for William Wilberforce's memorial in Westminster Abbey. Wilberforce is remembered for his work in abolishing slavery.

Trinity's library was designed free of charge by Sir Christopher Wren

The entrance steps to Trinity's Hall

Below: The Great Gate pre-dates Trinity as part of Edward III's King's Hall. It displays his sons' coats of arms. Henry VIII's statue presides over the entrance, his dignity only slightly diminished by the chair-leg given to him by students to serve as his sceptre. A toilet brush once appeared in its place, but the chair leg was swiftly reinstated.

TRINITY

How could King Henry VIII envisage anything but the grandest college in Cambridge? Such was his ambition when, in 1546, he began by amalgamating two existing colleges, Michaelhouse and King's Hall, with Physwick Hostel. With a Master, and sixty fellows and scholars, it was larger even than St. John's. Thomas Nevile's inspired designs included moving the entire clock tower 20 feet back to align with the chapel; today Great Court creates an awesome, dignified space that contrasts sharply with the crowded narrow street outside

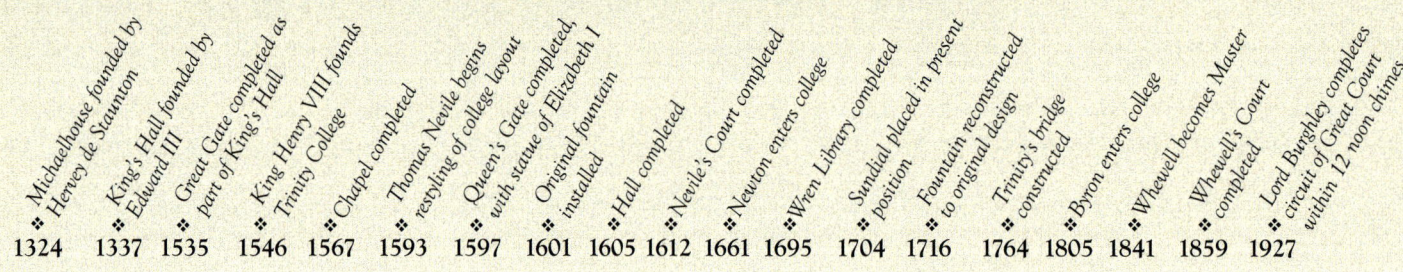

Left: Mild, modest Isaac Newton would have been familiar with Trinity's magnificent avenue of lime trees, first planted in 1672 and replanted in 1949. Newton published his 'Principia', which included his theory of gravity, in 1687. His former rooms are to the right of the Great Gate, viewed from the road, and the apple tree outside is descended from the famous tree that inspired him to that concept.

1324	1337	1535	1546	1567	1593	1597	1601	1605	1612	1661	1695	1704	1716	1764	1805	1841	1859	1927
Michaelhouse founded by Hervey de Staunton	King's Hall founded by Edward III	Great Gate completed as part of King's Hall	King Henry VIII founds Trinity College	Chapel completed	Thomas Nevile begins restyling of college layout	Queen's Gate completed, with statue of Elizabeth I	Original fountain installed	Hall completed	Nevile's Court completed	Newton enters college	Wren Library completed	Sundial placed in present position	Fountain reconstructed to original design	Trinity's bridge constructed	Byron enters college	Whewell becomes Master	Whewell's Court completed	Lord Burghley completes circuit of Great Court within 12 noon chimes

48

Trinity Bridge

The chapel, with its splendid painted ceiling, was finished in 1567. It contains statues of many Trinity men, including Newton, Tennyson, and the amazing Master William Whewell. This 'lion-like man', who funded Trinity's extension, Whewell's Court, could leap up the eight steps to the Hall in a single bound. He had no tolerance of loiterers on Trinity Bridge, but once met his match when he challenged an undergraduate, 'Sir, do you know what this bridge is for?' The answer, 'To go over it', to which he liked to exclaim, 'Then do so, sir!' did not come, however. This student was a Johnian who confounded him by saying, 'I understand this bridge was erected to give the best possible view of the New Buildings at St. John's'. But Whewell was sympathetic to the literary genius of Tennyson, who would read Virgil under the desk during Mathematics lectures. His unusually gentle call to order was, 'Mr. Tennyson, what's the compound interest of a penny put out at the Christian era up to the present time?' The stately Wren Library holds many precious manuscripts and early books, along with Lord Byron's statue. 'Mad, bad and dangerous to know', poet Byron tested college authority to the limit by keeping a bear and bathing in the fountain. The library also displays numerous portraits of men who have contributed to Trinity's illustrious history.

Overleaf: The cloisters of Nevile's Court were curtained off and used as a hospital during the First World War.

THE MARKET

Cambridge market established in its present location after the Great Fire of 1849. At this point the fountain head of Hobson's Conduit was moved to the corner of Lensfield Road. Until this time the market formed an L-shape around a group of houses destroyed by the fire. It sold a variety of produce including corn, poultry, milk and butter. The Cambridge tradition of selling butter by the yard: one pound rolled out to a strip one inch diameter, three feet long, continued until rationing in the First World War. The street name Peas Hill derives from the Latin *piscaria*: this was once the fish market. The story goes that on June 23rd 1626, a remarkable fish was bought here. A cod-fish, sold by a Mrs Brand, was cut open to be cleaned. To her amazement she found in its belly a book, wrapped in sail cloth. The event was witnessed by a University Bedell named Mr. Prime, who took the book to Dr. Gostling at Caius College.

Narrow streets extend from the market place. Rose Crescent was once the yard of the Rose Inn, where Samuel Pepys stayed several times. Petty Cury (meaning Little Cookery) was a quaint passageway with many cookery shops.

Two bronze tactile models of Cambridge, designed by Vernon McElroy, stand by Great St. Mary's. Commissioned by Rotary, they were unveiled in 2002 in commemoration of Queen Elizabeth II's Golden Jubilee.

Ladies of the town walked here at their peril at midday, when undergraduates enjoyed the sport of turning them upside down! It has been modernised beyond all recognition. Further changes are under way nearby. The demolition of the old Robert Sayle department store has made way for construction of the new 'Grand Arcade', and the newer shopping centre across Christ's Pieces at the Grafton Centre is growing in status.

Right: Cambridge Market Square

Above: Garret Hostel Lane. Cambridge's main trading place was originally not in the existing market, but on the land between the river and Queen's Road. The channels running at right angles from the river, such as that by Garret Hostel Lane, led to these former trading areas.

Until the railway arrived in 1845, the river Cam was a main artery of commerce for Cambridgeshire. The area by Silver Street bridge today throngs with punts in place of the congestion of barges that once packed the water. The maze of smaller waterways in this area would have led to mills and warehouses. King's Mill was first built by the infamous Sheriff Picot in Norman times and Bishop's Mill belonged to the Abbot of Ely. These mills were demolished in 1928.

As trade diminished, the water became purer and the twentieth century leisure activities of punting and rowing became more appealing. Cambridge was once famous for its trading fairs: Stourbridge Fair and Midsummer Fair were both widely acclaimed. Today's trend is, once more, to leisure. Midsummer Fair, which has been held in mid-June for 800 years, is now a major fun fair. Strawberry Fair is a popular annual festival of contemporary music and exotic clothing, art and jewellery stalls, and the Cambridge Folk Festival has become a music event of national importance.

Right: A summer evening near Silver Street Bridge with the spires of King's College chapel beyond.

The narrow streets of Cambridge are simply a pleasant place to take a walk. The unexpected quiet of these little lanes contrasts with the activity of the main streets, and reflects the academic nature of many residents. If it were not for the intrusion of the motor car, many streets would appear much as they did when they were built. There is a sense of timelessness, although there have been changes. The streets of Newnham, and the terraced houses around New Square, which once housed less well-off townspeople, have become highly desirable properties. Conversely, the orderly terraces of large Regency houses, close to the centre, were once residences for the richer citizens. Today they are often divided into flats to provide student accommodation or administrative centres for schools and colleges. Green spaces intermingled with the buildings create valuable havens for wildlife: areas such as St. Botolph's churchyard are deliberately allowed to grow as semi-wilderness.

Cambridge escaped serious wartime damage, although it sacrificed many iron railings to the war effort. It somehow evaded the intrusion of post-war high-rise buildings into its skyline. Cambridge has never been a centre for heavy industry. Recent years, however, have seen a new collaboration between the University and the business world. Cambridge's famous 'Silicon Fen' has become a major centre for technology and research since the foundation of the first science park in England by Trinity College in 1975. The city's success has created a demand for housing that today affects the whole county.

Above: The charming shutters, gas lamps, signs and worn paving-stones combine to create a civilised but slightly eccentric atmosphere that reveals many clues about the lives of bygone residents.

Left: Trinity Lane
Preceding Page: New Square, close to the city centre

The inns of Cambridge have played an important part in the life of the town. In the University's early years scholars sometimes took lodgings in them, and the traders and workmen along the river also benefited from their hospitality. Many provided accommodation for travellers by coach before the advent of the railway. Today many of the pubs in the centre of town have been modernised to create a more fashionable and exciting atmosphere. The oldest pub is said to be the 16th century Pickerel, close to Magdalene College, where Samuel Pepys was apt to drink through sermon time. The picturesque riverside pubs, the Green Dragon and the Fort St. George are of similar age. A sketch dated 1827 shows the Fort St. George was once on an island between the river and a channel to a lock. The Anchor by Silver Street Bridge is a great place to watch the punting activity nearby. The traditional atmosphere of an English pub is still found in many central pubs such as the Baron of Beef, the Mitre and the Free Press.

Left: The Eagle, owned by Corpus Christi, holds a poignant reminder of WW2 in the names of American airmen, written with candle smoke on the ceiling of the RAF Bar. A plaque records it as the place that Francis Crick and James Watson celebrated their discovery of the structure of DNA.

Overleaf: The Granta pub

HOBSON'S CONDUIT

The roadside channels that today trap unwary motorists along Trumpington Street were created almost 400 years ago. They are evidence of a network of watercourses fed from Nine Wells near the Gog Magog hills. These run along St. Andrew's Street, Trumpington Street, and to the Botanic Gardens. Cambridge benefited from its supply of clean water, brought to the fountain in the market square until alterations in 1849. The fountain was then moved to the corner of Lensfield Road where the water can sometimes be heard rushing under iron conduit covers. It was not solely the idea of Thomas Hobson, however. First proposed by Andrew Perne in 1574, it is a rare example of Town and Gown collaboration. Stephen Perse, of Caius College, brought the project together in 1604, at last providing fresh water to the plague-ridden town. Christ's College Fellows' swimming pool, and Emmanuel's ponds are both fed from its water supply.

Thomas Hobson was a key sponsor of the project. He kept a stables in what is now part of the grounds of St. Catharine's College, and one of the water channels ran conveniently past it. The famous saying, 'Hobson's choice, that or none', originated here: Hobson would only offer customers hire of the horse that had rested longest.

Hobson also contributed to Cambridge the 'Spinning House', a 'house of correction' for delinquent women. He may have been well-intentioned but the crowded conditions and over-zealous imprisonment of 'common women' brought it notoriety. At one point the Vice-Chancellor himself had to secure the release of 17 women incarcerated in a room only 19 feet square after others had died of fever! It was closed in 1894.

Left: A discreet iron conduit cover in the pavement near Christ's College
Opposite: Hobson's Conduit near the Botanic Gardens

'Reclining Figure' by Henry Moore, 1985

THE FITZWILLIAM MUSEUM

The Fitzwilliam Museum is named after Richard, 7th Viscount Fitzwilliam, who studied at Trinity Hall. He was a keen collector of art, and in 1816 he bequeathed his library, collection of paintings, and £100,000 to the University to build a place worthy of housing them. The collection has grown steadily, and today it is home to half a million treasures of national and international significance.

There is a substantial collection from Egypt, including a granite head of a Pharaoh from the Middle Kingdom, and a sarcophagus lid of Rameses III. The Roman and Greek artefacts are of special interest. There are also splendid exhibits of coins, ceramics, and textiles. The collection of ancient and modern manuscripts includes Keats' *Ode to a Nightingale*. It also holds a series of Handel manuscripts, and autographed compositions by Purcell, Bach and Mozart. The range of art is extensive. Works from Rembrandt and Reubens to Picasso and Barbara Hepworth, may be enjoyed, along with numerous old master drawings, watercolours and engravings. The collection is constantly evolving through bequests and purchases and it regularly hosts additional visiting collections. The displays are being made ever more accessible and exciting, and the friendly museum staff are always pleased to provide further information.

The building itself deserves as much attention as its contents. Its magnificent Corinthian façade is an imposing feature of Trumpington Street, guarded by four huge stone lions. The foundation stone was laid in 1837, and the first architect was George Basevi, who fell to his death from scaffolding at Ely Cathedral before its completion. The work was continued by C.R. Cockerell, who designed the impressive bronze doors and ornate gates. A single visit to the Fitzwilliam cannot fully do justice to what has been described as 'One of the greatest art collections of the nation and a monument of the first importance'.

Right: The imposing Museum entrance

Cambridge's churches are richly varied, ranging from miniature St. Andrew's on Castle Hill to the splendour of the Catholic Church near Parker's Piece. The University's official place of worship is Great St. Mary's, which might be considered the heart of Cambridge, as it is also the starting point for the measurement of milestones along the London road. A church has existed here since 1205, but this structure was begun in 1478, following a fire. The tower was added in 1608. Its builder, John Warren, is commemorated inside: sadly, he fell from the tower to his death on the day of its completion. Safety measures today prevent further tragedy; for the athletic, this point offers one of the finest views of the city.

Left: Great St. Mary's Church

Below Left: The Round Church, the Church of the Holy Sepulchre is based on the church of the same name in Jerusalem. It is the oldest out of only four such buildings in the country, dating from the early 12th century. Before 1841, the belfry was octagonal, but was altered during restoration. Inside, eight Norman arches surround the circular centre, supported by massive pillars decorated with intriguing carved stone faces.

Overleaf: The view from Great St. Mary's

St. Benedict's, often known as St. Bene't's, was used by Corpus Christi College until the 17th century. Its Saxon tower dates from 1025. It is possible that this tower was the first in the country to ring out an organised peal: its parish clerk, Fabian Stedman, is said to have devised the system of 'change-ringing' in the 1670s. The church is also the burial place of the famous carrier, Thomas Hobson, who presented a bible which is now displayed here.

THE BOTANIC GARDENS

The first Botanic Garden was founded in 1762. It was originally set closer to the centre of Cambridge, designed along the lines of the Physic Garden at Chelsea to educate medical students in the uses of plants. It was Steven Henslow, a dedicated botanist and teacher of Charles Darwin, who initiated the move to the Gardens' present location on Trumpington Street, with a new site acquired from Trinity Hall in 1831. By this time overseas exploration was bringing to light an exciting variety of exotic plants, and Henslow persuaded the University that much could be gained from study of the plants themselves, beyond their medicinal properties. The current Gardens were opened on November 2nd, 1846.

The Main Walk, with its magnificent coniferous trees, the lake, Systematic Beds and winding path around the circumference are still in place. The Gardens are evolving to this day; they hold international status as a centre for all aspects of botanical research. They also supply data on the weather to the Meteorological Office at Bracknell. They are constantly evolving: many of the recent garden areas are focused on aspects of climate change, ecology and sustainable horticulture. The Gardens have a policy of using a minimum of irrigation or artificial fertilizers. As many different environments as possible are represented, with about 8000 species of plants, 2000 of which are held in the Glasshouse Range.

The Gardens' main purpose is scientific study, but their aesthetic appeal will enchant visitors of all ages. Even in the depths of winter there are areas filled with colour, scent and a wonderful tapestry of natural forms. The Glasshouses recreate the atmospheres of jungle, desert and alpine conditions in a fabulous and imaginatively displayed range of exhibits. Whether you choose to wander for hours through the grounds, or find a shady sanctuary to rest and absorb the peace, the Botanic Gardens are a perennial joy.

Left: The Palm House contains many fascinating tropical species.
Overleaf: The Botanic Gardens are a pot-pourri of sensory delight.

PETERHOUSE

Most ancient of the colleges, Peterhouse was founded in 1284 when Bishop Hugh de Balsham's attempt to integrate his 'lay ecclesiastical' scholars alongside the brethren at the Hospital of St. John proved unworkable. His new establishment emulated 'the Oxford Scholars of Merton, studiously engaged in the pursuit of literature'. 'Literature' here referred to learning in the context of theological study rather than the modern interpretation of English literature. College rules were strict: scholars wore the 'tonsure' of the monks and attended chapel frequently. The college long held connections with the Bishops of Ely. Its ancient wall enclosing the 'deer-park' has a doorway bearing the crests of two early bishops who, in the days of the waterlogged fens coming right up to the wall, would visit by boat.

Peterhouse has had its share of troubled times. Master Andrew Perne had no time for 'the names of partialities, sects or divisions, either in civil or religious causes' which he viewed as 'but foolish words or petting terms'. During the ebb and flow of political tides in the 16th century he simply adopted the view of the moment, ensuring not only his own job security but that of the college. The luck could not hold under Parliamentarian rule, however. Infamous Dowsing, sent by Cromwell to scourge the colleges of papist idolatry, destroyed around 100 carved angels in the chapel and smashed all the stained glass except the east window, which the fellows had managed to conceal in time.

Peterhouse has nurtured many scientific innovators, including Cockerell, Whittle, Babbage and Cavendish. Although brilliant, Cavendish's shy nature caused him to fail his exams when he dared not speak in front of his professors.

Right: The archway in Old Court leads to Gisborne Court and the gardens.

Peterhouse chapel is affectionately referred to as 'the grandfather clock' because of its distinctive shape. It was begun in 1632 while Matthew Wren, Uncle of Sir Christopher Wren, was Master. Matthew Wren was also Bishop of Ely and later became Master of Pembroke College as well. He is remembered as a capable leader of Peterhouse. It is recorded that he

'built great part of the College from the ground, rescued their Writings and Records from the Dust and Worms, and by indefatigable industry digested them with a good Method and Order'

Things may have slackened somewhat by 1710 when the German bibliographer Uffenbach visited the college. Not only did he comment that the manuscripts there were 'sorry stuff', but they were so encrusted with dust that he had to wear a pinafore while the librarian cleaned them with a towel.

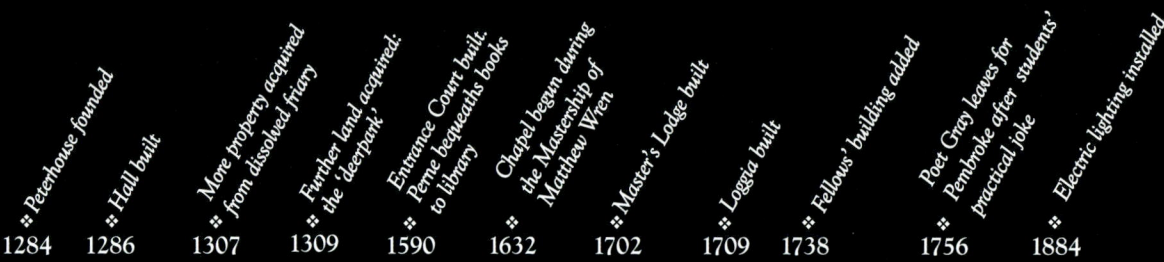

1284	1286	1307	1309	1590	1632	1702	1709	1738	1756	1884
Peterhouse founded	Hall built	More property acquired from dissolved friary	Further land acquired: the 'deerpark'	Entrance Court built. Perne bequeaths books to library	Chapel begun during the Mastership of Matthew Wren	Master's Lodge built	Loggia built	Fellows' building added	Poet Gray leaves for Pembroke after students' practical joke	Electric lighting installed

Lord Kelvin was a fellow of Peterhouse. In 1884, to mark the 600th anniversary, he was responsible for the installation of electric lighting: the first college to do so. This luxury did not meet entirely with approval, however. The college laundresses are said to have been enraged by the damage done to their clean washing by smuts from the new generator.

Overleaf: Peterhouse experiences a kind of natural illumination in springtime. The 'deerpark', where deer were kept until the 1930s, is filled with a dazzling carpet of daffodils, which surpasses any other Cambridge college garden.

CLARE

It is a favourite Cambridge challenge to invite visitors to count the number of stone balls adorning Clare Bridge, the answer being not 14, as it first appears, but thirteen and four fifths! Several stories surround the origin of one ball's missing segment, but the most probable is builder Thomas Grumbold's revenge for the college's underpayment of only three shillings.

The college's quiet, refined atmosphere was once enlivened by a spider's web suspended over Old Court, made from over a mile of string, complete with a giant spider named 'Arabella' by its student creators. Further student creativity may be enjoyed each summer with plays set in the college's splendid gardens. Drama has long been enjoyed here. In James I's time, the college staged 'Club Law', a parody of the town's dignitaries, intended to infuriate the townspeople who were invited and then 'riveted in with scholars on all sides' to endure the spectacle.

Above: The chapel and lantern in Old Court
Left: Clare's beautiful, 'incomplete' bridge

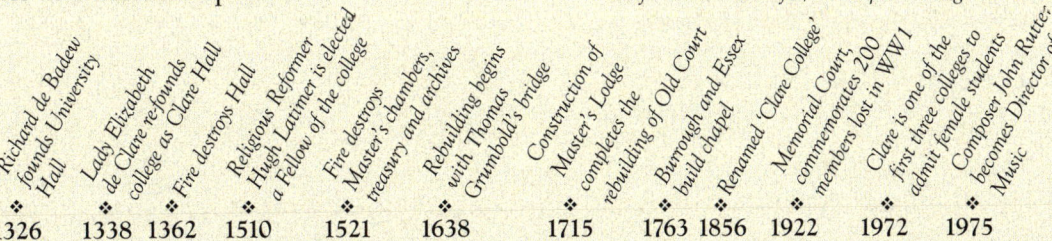

Richard de Badew founds University Hall	Lady Elizabeth de Clare refounds college as Clare Hall	Fire destroys Hall	Religious Reformer Hugh Latimer is elected a Fellow of the college	Fire destroys Master's chambers, treasury and archives	Rebuilding begins with Thomas Grumbold's bridge	Construction of Master's Lodge completes the rebuilding of Old Court	Burrough and Essex build chapel	Renamed 'Clare College'	Memorial Court, commemorates 200 members lost in WW1	Clare is one of the first three colleges to admit female students	Composer John Rutter becomes Director of Music
1326	1338	1362	1510	1521	1638	1715	1763	1856	1922	1972	1975

Right:
Immaculate
topiary in Clare
gardens with
King's Gibbs
Building beyond.

Overleaf:
The stunning
riverside Fellows'
Garden is
overlooked by
Trinity Hall's
library.

Clare's wrought
iron gates are a
specially elegant
feature.

Lady Elizabeth de Clare came to the financial rescue of Richard de Badew's University Hall in 1338, forty years after the University first acquired the site. She turned to charitable works having been three times widowed; her shield's black border with golden tears allude to her bereavement. Her purpose in re-founding the college was replacement of clergy lost to the Black Death. Even with her assistance the college struggled financially, with only two chairs, one jug and two basins to be shared by the thirty or so early members! It owes a debt of gratitude to Nicholas Ridley for countering its proposed amalgamation with Trinity Hall in 1548. Further troubles beset it in the form of two fires. Its slow phoenix-like recovery began in 1638 with the building of Cambridge's first stone bridge, which served both to transport building materials across the river and as an access avoiding the plague-ridden town. Cromwell hindered progress by requisitioning its stone to fortify the castle. Building resumed with the combined contributions of James Essex and William Burrough, ultimately creating a harmonious structure 'more like a palace than a college'.

PEMBROKE

Marie de Saint Pol, Countess of Pembroke, was a close friend of Elizabeth of Clare. Perhaps it was her example that inspired Marie to create this, the third oldest Cambridge college, founded in 1347. It soon established a reputation for good character and learning, and benefited from Henry VI's financial assistance. The wise lady showed great foresight in ensuring that it had all the facilities needed to operate as an independent establishment, including the innovative asset of its own chapel. It won the respect of Queen Elizabeth I, who proclaimed it *'O domus antiqua et religiosa!'* on her visit to Cambridge. It has been a peaceful place of learning for imaginative, creative and visionary people throughout its history. Religious reformer Nicholas Ridley wrote of it lovingly prior to his execution, poets Thomas Gray, Edmund Spenser and Ted Hughes flourished here, and Prime Minister William Pitt entered the college aged only 13. In the 1700s, Dr. Long constructed an ingenious device called the 'planetarium': a metal globe model illustrating the movements of the planets. He was also noted for his invention of a water 'velocipede' which he used to ride on the 'water works' he had created. John Couch Adams, co-discoverer of Neptune, was a fellow here. Pembroke suffered greater loss than any other college in the First World War, when one fifth of its serving members perished. Happier times more recently have nurtured the gentle wit and humour of Bill Oddie and Tim Brooke-Taylor.

1347	❖	Hall of Valence Marie founded
1452	❖	Library added above Hall
1540	❖	Nicholas Ridley becomes Master
1569	❖	Edmund Spenser matriculates
1605	❖	Matthew Wren elected fellow
1614	❖	Second court begun
1665	❖	Consecration of new chapel, designed by Sir Christopher Wren
1690	❖	Old chapel converted to library
1712	❖	Trumpington Street side refaced
1756	❖	Thomas Gray migrates
1773	❖	William Pitt attends college
1875	❖	Waterhouse demolishes old Hall. His new buildings included a Library, Hall and Master's Lodge
1924	❖	War Memorial dedicated to Pembroke members lost in WW1
1931	❖	Ghandi stays at the college
1957	❖	'Orchard Building' completed
1998	❖	Foundress Court opened by the Chancellor

90

Thomas Gray took refuge at Pembroke after an unhappy time at Peterhouse. Rev. John Sharp records on March 12, 1756,

'This case is much talked of, and is this. He is much afraid of fire ... he has ever since kept a ladder of rope by him, soft as the silky cords by which Romeo ascended to his Juliet, and has had an iron machine fixed to his bedroom window. The other morning, Lord Percival and some Petrucheans, going a hunting ... thought it would be no bad diversion to make Gray bolt, as they called it, so ordered their man Joe Draper to roar out fire. A delicate white nightcap is said to have appeared at the window: but finding the mistake, retired again to the couch. The young fellows, had he descended, were determined, they said, to have whipped the butterfly up again'.

Gray confides to a friend on March 25:

'I left my lodgings because the rooms were noisy, and the People of the house dirty... All I shall say more is, that I am for the present extremely well lodged here, and as quiet as in the Grand Chartreuse; and that everybody ... are as civil as they could be to Mary de Valence in person'.

Overleaf: Pembroke's meticulously tended grounds have a beautiful display of summer colour.

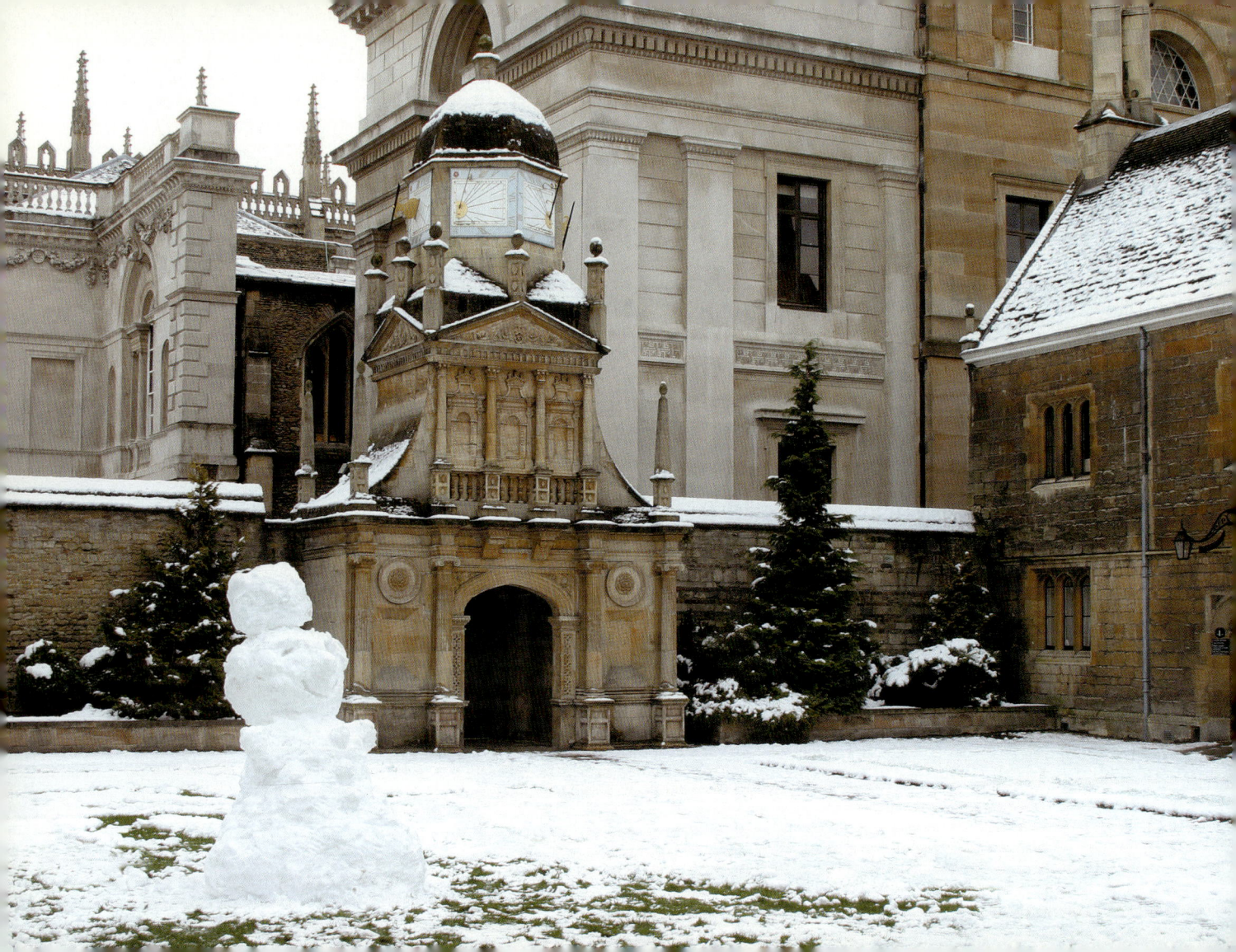

GONVILLE AND CAIUS

Above: The statue of Dr. Stephen Perse, who was a major benefactor to the college. The building he holds represents the school he also bequeathed funds for in 1615.

Gonville and Caius' distinctive Gothic tower dominates the end of King's Parade, and carved faces of its bygone fellows watch over passers by in Trinity Street. Originally founded by Edmund Gonville, and rescued from financial ruin by his friend William Bateman, it was later re-established by Dr. John Keys, who upgraded his name to a Latinised form after returning from medical studies abroad. Caius was a singular character: highly accomplished, dedicated to the pursuit of excellence, and intolerant of shortcomings. His first statutes, created long before today's political correctness, forbade the election of scholars who were 'deaf, dumb, deformed, lame, confirmed invalids or Welshmen'! He remained staunchly Catholic among his reformed Puritan colleagues. In 1572 some of the fellows, authorised by Vice-Chancellor Thomas Bynge, raided his rooms of his Catholic 'College Treasures'. Caius himself records,

> *'Outrageously he treated them, cutting them in pieces, casting them on the fire, and assailing them with horrible names and epithets ... what they could not burn they broke and defaced with hammers'.*

There is a wealth of architectural interest and scientific achievement at the college. Architect William Wilkins studied here. William Harvey's theory of the circulation of blood, James Chadwick's discovery of the neutron, and John Venn's mathematical diagram, all originated at Caius. The college has more recently nurtured Stephen Hawking's outstanding work on theoretical physics.

Dr. Caius built three symbolic gates. The 'Gate of Humility', now simply reading, 'Humilitatis', suggests the proper attitude with which to enter. His 'Gate of Virtue' provides a constant reminder to study diligently, and scholars depart triumphantly through his ornate 'Gate of Honour'.

Left: Caius Court and Gate of Honour

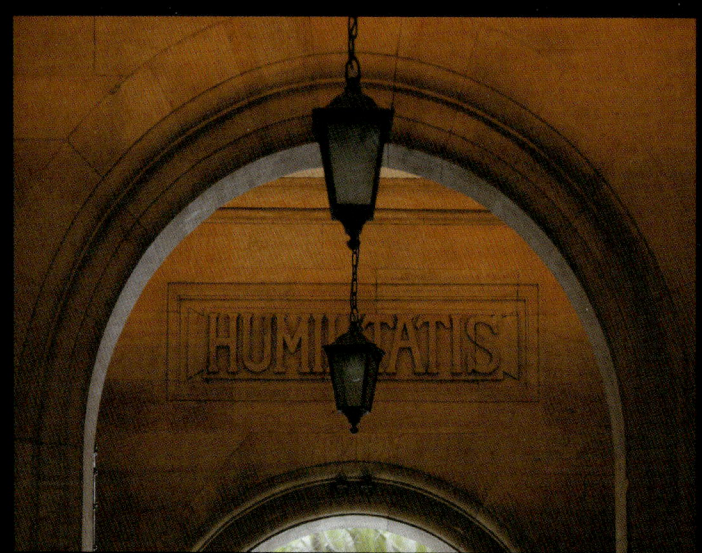

The Gate of Humility

Nov. 3rd, 1693: 'This day I beheld a strange experiment ...one amongst us, a musitioner, told us that he would shew us a strange thing. So the before say'd fellow led us to that exceedingly strong quadrangular portico of Kaius Colledge, that looks towards the publick schools. And when we got there he began to sing the note of a dubble "do, soh, re", which he had no sooner sounded but that the whole portico manifestly and visibly trembled as if there had been a kind of earthquake.... This is a property that has been observed to be in this portico this hundred years together'.

Right: The Gate of Honour in Senate House Passage, with Trinity Hall beyond

Edmund Gonville founds Gonville Hall — 1348

William Bateman, Bishop of Norwich, takes over development of college — 1351

Chapel building commences — 1353

John Keys, later Caius, enters college as a student — 1529

Caius refounds college as Gonville and Caius — 1557

Caius resigns and dies — 1573

Burrough improves buildings in Gonville Court — 1751

Hall completed by Salvin — 1854

Tree Court building replaced by Waterhouse — 1868

Dr. Wilson takes college flag on Scott's ill-faced Antarctic expedition — 1912

Athlete Harold Abrahams, depicted in the film 'Chariots of Fire', admitted to Caius — 1919

1st and only Oxford/ Cambridge air race won by Caius' W. Philcox — 1921

Development of Harvey Court on West Road — 1960

TRINITY HALL

The Black Death had no respect for morality. In 1350 it had all but wiped out Bishop William Bateman's clergy in Norfolk, and he took steps to remedy the matter. Three years earlier he had acquired the monks of Ely's hostel in Cambridge as a gift from John de Crawden, and here he founded Trinity Hall, not only to replace his clergy but to provide trained logicians who could support papal authority. His stipulation that a minimum of 10 out his initial 20 fellows should be civilian was unpopular among some, as was anything that challenged Church authority at that time, but the college flourished nonetheless. Lord Chesterfield was later to remark that it was 'the best in all the University' and 'full of lawyers who have lived in the world and know how to behave.'

The name has sometimes been understandably confused with Trinity College. Its history dates back to the days when 'college' meant the body of people at the establishment, and 'hall' referred to the building, hence the early names Clare Hall, King's Hall etc. By the time this trend was changing, Henry VIII had already founded Trinity College, so 'Trinity Hall' had to remain unaltered. The lawyers from the college travelled to London a great deal, and in 1730, Dr. William Mowse funded the first milestones since Roman occupation, which may still be seen, bearing the college crest, along Trumpington Road.

Trinity Hall's distinctive crest

Left: Trinity Hall's appearance belies it true age due to eighteenth century stone refacing but, in the passage to B staircase, the original 14th century stone remains. Outside in Garret Hostel Lane, the walls have brick facing for a different reason: in the days of land by the river being used for grazing, frequent traffic of livestock along the lane was seriously eroding the original stone clunch of the former monks' hostel.

The rules regarding socialising with women have always been strict. In 1930, the bursar of Trinity Hall fined an undergraduate a whole pound, three times the norm, for giving his gown to a girlfriend.

'6/8´ for not wearing your gown, 6/8´ for giving it to someone who is not a member of the University, and 6/8´ for not having better taste in young women.'

Trinity Hall's ancient Elizabethan library houses a special collection of books, including a work by Erasmus, published in 1521 by the first Cambridge printer, John Siberch.

1350 ❖ Bateman founds college

1366 ❖ Chapel commenced

1730 ❖ College provides milestones

1761 ❖ Museum founder Viscount Fitzwilliam attends college

1794 ❖ Composition of chimes for Great St. Mary's

1850 ❖ Fire destroys east side First Court

1852 ❖ Salvin rebuilds First Court

1898 ❖ Electric lighting installed

1935 ❖ North Court added

1956 ❖ Robert Runcie is college Dean

1977 ❖ The college admits female students

1998 ❖ Jerwood Library built

The gardens at tiny Trinity Hall encapsulate the old-world charm that pervades many of Cambridge's ancient places. They are especially lovely in high summer, with the blazing colours of the herbaceous borders. The fellows' garden, glimpsed through a wrought iron gate which was formerly the dining hall entrance, contains massive chestnut trees, over 200 years old, which are spectacular at any time.

Trinity Hall's 'unadventurous stability' has produced achievements much greater than its size. As Bateman intended, it has remained a stronghold for the legal profession. The college's proximity to the river may account for its regular success in rowing. Trinity Hall had no organ until 1922, but it has also made a world-famous musical contribution in the form of the 'Westminster chimes', for Great St. Mary's church. These may be attributed either to William Crotch, a musical prodigy, or his tutor Dr. Jowett, who was also a talented musician at the college.

The new Jerwood library, standing tall over the river, is said to be designed with the structure of a ship in mind. It is certainly an inspiring place to study, overlooking the beautiful gardens of Clare College. It goes as far as to provide beds for dedicated students who wish to study deep into the night!

1352	❖	Guilds found college
1381	❖	College almost destroyed in Peasant's Revolt
1544	❖	Reformer Archbishop Matthew Parker becomes Master
1575	❖	Matthew Parker dies
1581	❖	Christopher Marlowe enters college
1662	❖	New chapel completed
1710	❖	German bibliographer Uffenbach is impressed by the college's library
1827	❖	New Court, designed by William Wilkins, completed
1891	❖	Lewis Collection of coins and gems etc. bequeathed by Rev. S. S. Lewis
1919	❖	Old Court restored by T.H. Lyon
1953	❖	A painting, dated 1585, discovered during renovation: thought possibly to be of Marlowe
1983	❖	College admits female students

CORPUS CHRISTI

In 1352 the ravages of plague provoked the townspeople to create a college to replace their lost priests. The united guilds of Corpus Christi and St. Mary built close to St. Bene't's church. For a long time this was the college place of worship and many people referred to it as 'Bene't's College'. Corpus is notable for having been founded independent of University initiative, so it is paradoxical that this college should bear the brunt of the Peasants' Revolt of 1381, when many treasures and parchments were stolen and burnt in the market place. An old woman named Margaret Sterr is said to have thrown the ashes in the air, declaring, 'Thus, thus let the learning of all scholars be confounded!' The scholars persevered, of course. Corpus' superb collection of ancient manuscripts, given to the college by Matthew Parker, today includes St. Augustine's 6th century Gospel Book and King Alfred's copy of the Anglo-Saxon Chronicle.

Image courtesy: The Master & Fellows of Corpus Christi College Cambridge

Plague struck again in the 1630s. Henry Butts, Master, bravely remained to tend the sick when many others had fled, but the horror drove him to suicide. His ghost is said to frequent the college. The poet and playwright Marlowe is commemorated here: his dramatic skill also qualified him as a spy for Elizabeth 1 against the papists: one of the first recruited at Cambridge.

Marlowe's Memorial

Above: Medieval Old Court is the most ancient in Cambridge: Its only rival is at Queens'. A Pelican in the corner marks the rooms of Archbishop Parker.

Opposite: William Wilkins designed New Court: a plan by Essex, intended to reflect the three-sided court of St. Catharine's, was never used. Wilkins' Gothic style in the street front and chapel are almost a cameo of the greater examples at nearby King's.

Right: St. Catharine's is known affectionately as 'St. Catz'.

ST. CATHARINE'S

Left: The dignified symmetry of St. Catharine's court is the work of Robert Grumbold, son of the designer of Clare Bridge. It echoes the strong, elegant style of his work in the Wren Bridge at St. John's.

The college crest is the wheel of mythical St. Catharine of Alexandria. Condemned to be put to death on its spikes, her sanctity is said to have caused it to break asunder.

St. Catharine's was founded in 1473 by Robert Wodelark, third Provost of King's. Established for the study of theology and philosophy by qualified academics, its focus was purely religious, with medicine and law studies expressly forbidden. There were no undergraduates for 100 years and financial necessity may have driven it to admit students. The college was poor enough to deserve special concessions when town fire precautions were reviewed in 1575. Most colleges were required to provide four fire buckets, but St. Catharine's and Magdalene were asked for just two. Its fortunes improved in the 1700s when John Eachard instigated its renovation, and it received a considerable bequest in 1745 from Mary Ramsden. Its most significant alumnus must be John Addenbrooke in 1697, who is renowned for his establishment of Cambridge's magnificent hospital. His medicine chest is still kept by the college. Recent alumni include Sir Peter Hall and Jeremy Paxman.

JESUS COLLEGE

The narrow walled path leading to Jesus College is known as 'The Chimney'. It approaches an impressive gate-tower, from which the founder's statue looks down on visitors. A moment's consideration of the crest, a cockerel perched on a globe, will explain his name: John Alcock, once Bishop of Ely. He founded the college in 1496, but Jesus College's origins date back over 800 years, to when an order of Benedictine nuns, the Priory of St. Mary and St. Radegund, was created in 1138. Their earliest surviving charter, given by Nigel, Bishop of Ely, dates from the mid 1140s, and their chapel was built on land granted by King Malcolm of Scotland in around 1157. It is possible that Bishop Alcock planned his college several years in advance, allowing the number of nuns to dwindle by ceasing to admit new members. The nuns' reputation has suffered from tales surrounding the nature of their order's decline, ranging from their 'dissolute disposition' to accusations of promiscuity. Their life was indisputably hard: only one fire was allowed in the whole establishment, in the 'warming room', and the inmates were restricted in the time they could spend there.

The college buildings have evolved over the years, with special embellishments in the chapel from William Morris' firm. There remains an enduring sense of calm and the weight of many years filling the shadowy cloisters, and the vast open spaces are a surprise so close to the city centre. The modern sculptures in the grounds complement the curious natural forms of the topiary yew trees, and in spring the lawns are scattered with bright crocus.

The original church and buildings exceeded Alcock's requirements for his college of a Master, six fellows and a moderate number of scholars; he modified them considerably. Three beautiful arches, (left), dating from around 1210, were discovered during alterations in 1893. They are the remains of the entrance to the Priory's Chapter-house.

The poet Samuel Taylor Coleridge spent a rather erratic time at Jesus. At one point he ran away to enlist as a soldier, only to return after a less than successful military experience. Apparently his skill with words did not extend to such matters as staying mounted on a horse. During his ensuing punishment by the college, being 'gated', he wrote to a friend,

'The confinement is nothing. I have the fields and the grove to walk in, and what can I wish for more?'

Left: The 'Chimney' and gate-tower, with Bishop Alcock's statue

Right: Morgan Avenue in spring time
Overleaf: Wisteria in Outer Court

EMMANUEL

Queen Elizabeth I: 'I hear, Sir Walter, that you have erected a Puritan foundation'
Sir Walter Mildmay: 'I have only set an acorn, which, when it becomes an oak, God alone
knows what will be the fruit thereof'.

This enterprising move by Sir Walter was to produce free thinking 'fruit' that shaped not only England's future but spread seedlings across the Atlantic to newly discovered America. His foundation rose out of the site of the former Dominican 'preaching' friars' monastery. As the name suggests, Christianity was a primary focus of the college. Moreover, Mildmay intended to send the word of God far afield, stipulating that, 'We would not have any Fellow suppose that we have given him in this College a perpetual abode'.

Mildmay's objective was to produce preaching ministers for the Church of England. His views on discipline were formidably strict, frowning on feasting, playing and talking, and requiring regular inspection of scholars' chambers. In addition there were the frequent chapel attendances, nightly prayers by the tutor and extra Sunday lectures on the Christian faith. The addresses of first Master Laurence Chaderton seem to have been popular, though. It is said that when he showed signs of ending a two hour sermon, the congregation implored, 'For God's sake, sir, go on!' In the 1630s this religious fervour inspired 35 Emmanuel men to set sail for America to spread the word of the Gospel. John Harvard, who bequeathed his library and half his estate to America's first university, was among them. Sir Walter's reassurance to the Queen may have been eloquently neutral, but the north-south orientation of the chapel suggested a rejection of Catholic ideals. The college was favoured by Cromwell's regime because it was Puritan: during the 1640s eight Masters imposed on other colleges came from Emmanuel.

The Wren Chapel invites comparison with that of Peterhouse. It was initiated by William Sancroft in 1668, is once more aligned east-west to remove 'the former singularity which rendered us heretofore so unhappily remarkable'. Its chandelier dates from 1732, and the altar piece by Giacomo Amiconi was presented in 1734.

Left: The interior of the Wren Chapel

Samuel Parr, also known as 'Whig Johnson' may have been showing the influence of his college environment in his response to the suggestion that it was a woman's privilege to talk nonsense.

'No, Madame, it is not their privilege but their infirmity. Ducks would walk if they could, but nature suffers them only to waddle'.

Opposite: Emmanuel's tranquil gardens are especially lovely in spring.

Overleaf: Paddock's Pond was once the Dominican monks' fishpond. Today it is the home of Emmanuel's colourful collection of ducks.

Emmanuel men's explorations were not restricted to the geographical sense. Studies in anatomy were also a focus. In the 1780s Sir Busick Harwood, later 1st Professor of Medicine at Downing, amassed a gruesome set of tales. These were ghastly enough to induce an attack of nausea in the geologist Adam Sedgwick that forced him to dismount his horse.

Friary dissolved	Emmanuel founded	John Harvard enters college	Brick building begun	Harvard emigrates	Wren Chapel built, Mildmay's chapel becomes library	Westmorland Building added	James Essex adds buildings to Front Court	New Court added	8 Tercentenary stained glass windows added to chapel: one commemorates Harvard	Mildmay's original chapel converted from library to dining hall
536	1584	1627	1633	1637	1677	1718	1770	1824	1884	1930

MAGDALENE

Magdalene College, by the site of the original 'Great Bridge', is the only college set entirely on the far side of the river. It began as a monastic hostel, well suited to educational purposes. The Dukes of Buckingham funded much of its early development and it was known as Buckingham College until 1542, when Henry VIII dissolved the monasteries. Lord Chancellor Thomas Audley refounded it as 'The College of St. Mary Magdalene'. Audley presided over the trial of John Fisher, and had a reputation for ruthlessness. It was said of his gravestone that, 'The stone is not harder nor the marble blacker than the heart of him who lies beneath'. The pronunciation of Magdalene as 'Maudlin' follows his wish that it should sound like his name. Mastership of the college was traditionally nominated by the 'Visitor', a title accompanying ownership of Audley End at Saffron Walden. The college motto *'Garde ta Foy'*, (Keep your faith), is sometimes humorously interpreted as 'Mind your liver!' Magdalene is still renowned for its candlelit Hall. Drink has been both enjoyed and frowned upon. Samuel Pepys, upbraided by the college himself for his excesses, writes of his shame at being seen with his red-nosed friend, Master John Peachell. This unfortunate gentleman abstained from his beloved liquor for four days after a college reprimand, and thus perished. By the late 1700s, however, Evangelical students insisted on tea so successfully that by Magdalene the river Cam was 'rendered unnavigable by tea-leaves'.

Opposite: Graduation Day. Magdalene students process through the town to Senate House for their graduation ceremony.

Below: Magdalene guards a special treasure in the Pepys Library. Samuel Pepys bequeathed his superb collection of books and diaries to the college. The volumes were to be kept as a unit and inspected annually. If any discrepancy occurred, they were to be entrusted to Trinity College instead. Until the 1930s, the students enjoyed a summertime tradition of sleeping out under its elegant cloisters.

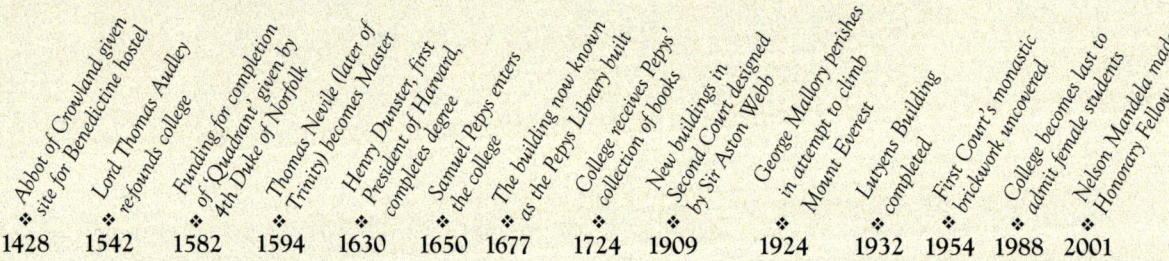

Left: The distinctive, rich coloured brickwork of medieval First Court was uncovered in 1954. Monastic coats of arms are visible over the doorways.

Opposite: The timbered house in Benson Court is part of a complex of buildings adapted when the college expanded across the road in the early 1920s. Funds were tight, and baths were nearly dismissed as 'unnecessary luxury' in the new accommodation!

Abbot of Crowland given
site for Benedictine hostel
❖ 1428

Lord Thomas Audley
refounds college
❖ 1542

Funding for completion
of 'Quadrant' given by
4th Duke of Norfolk
1582

Thomas Nevile (later of
Trinity) becomes Master
1594

Henry Dunster, first
President of Harvard,
completes degree
1630

Samuel Pepys enters
the college
1650

The building now known
as the Pepys Library built
1677

College receives Pepys'
collection of books
❖ 1724

New buildings in
Second Court designed
by Sir Aston Webb
1909

George Mallory perishes
in attempt to climb
Mount Everest
❖ 1924

Lutyens Building
completed
❖ 1932

First Court's monastic
brickwork uncovered
1954

College becomes last to
admit female students
1988

Nelson Mandela made
Honorary Fellow
2001

SIDNEY SUSSEX

*'There is a little College just beside a busy street,
It's name is Sidney Sussex and you'll find it hard to beat'*

This charming college, tucked discreetly behind a high wall in Sidney Street, was founded in 1596 at the bequest of Frances, Countess of Sussex, daughter of Sir William Sidney. Like Emmanuel and Jesus, it had monastic connections as the site of the former Franciscan friary. Despite the University's eagerness to acquire it, this had been dismantled to a great extent in Henry VIII's time, to provide building material for his own pride and joy, Trinity College. Queen Elizabeth finally asserted control of the situation and granted a charter for purchase of the land in 1594.

Lady Frances left funds in her will that she had carefully set aside for the project, but even in the 16th century it was a scanty provision. The writer Thomas Fuller remarked, 'We usually observe infants born in the seventh month, though poor and pitiful creatures, are vital, and, with great care and good attendance, in time prove proper persons. Alas! What is five thousand pounds to buy the site, build and endow a College therewith?' Nevertheless, the executors proved themselves capable of nurturing the college in its infancy, creating, as Lady Frances wished, 'a godlie moniment for the mainteynance of good learninge'.

In the shelter of the footstep-hollowed cloisters, the constant stream of shoppers just the other side of the wall passes almost unnoticed. Sidney Sussex's carefully tended grounds, with their tall trees and partitions of shrubbery, are a green sanctuary which maintains the air of a country garden. The occasional sculptures set within the grounds are an additional delight. Even the austerity of the courtyards, designed in emulation of Gonville and Caius, is softened by a variety of climbing plants. In June the ancient wisteria is especially impressive.

Left: Cloister Court

Jeffery Wyatt's architectural additions (right) conceal the original red brick walls beneath distinctive gables and Roman cement facing. His style was much favoured by George IV, who commissioned him for improvements to Windsor Castle and knighted him Sir Jeffery Wyattville.

Opposite: Sidney Sussex's idyllic gardens

S idney Sussex's most notable student is Oliver Cromwell, who entered the college on the same day Shakespeare died: St. George's Day, April 23rd, 1616. He only stayed for one year, leaving when his father died, and it seems there was not time for any bond of affection to develop. During the Civil War the college sent £100 to assist the king, and the elderly Master Samuel Ward was arrested by the Parliamentarians. Despite their historical differences, Cromwell's head has been returned for burial at the college, and his famous 'warts and all' portrait is also housed here.

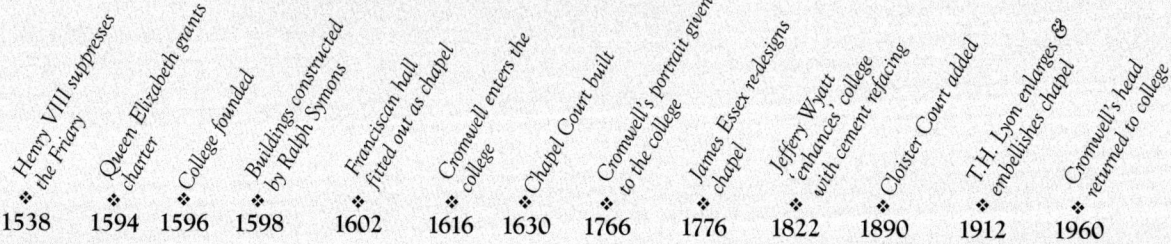

Henry VIII suppresses the Friary	Queen Elizabeth grants charter	College founded	Buildings constructed by Ralph Symons	Franciscan hall fitted out as chapel	Cromwell enters the college	Chapel Court built	Cromwell's portrait given to the college	James Essex re-designs chapel	Jeffery Wyatt 'enhances' college with cement refacing	Cloister Court added	T.H. Lyon enlarges & embellishes chapel	Cromwell's head returned to college
1538	1594	1596	1598	1602	1616	1630	1766	1776	1822	1890	1912	1960

DOWNING

Visitors entering through Downing College's narrow gate on Regent Street might be forgiven for thinking they have stepped across the Atlantic into an American college campus. Its buildings have evolved around extensive lawns and avenues which rival Trinity for spaciousness. However, William Wilkins envisaged this design long before any such thing was conceived in America's first college sites. Downing's unique neo-classical architecture signified a new chapter in the life of the University. Here was the first college foundation since Sidney Sussex in 1596. Set apart from its predecessors not only in appearance, but also in purpose, it was the first college to be founded independent of an existing religious building. However, Wilkins' original grand intentions were never fully realised. Protracted legal battles diverted much of Sir George Downing's original bequest into the pockets of the lawyers between his last heir's death in 1764 and the laying of the first stone in 1807. It is perhaps fitting that law is still one of the specialisms of the college.

The Downing name is also immortalised in the London address of Britain's Prime Minister: this land was once property of the Downing family. Their financial success far outweighed their popularity. Sir George's grandfather was notorious for his deceptions between Charles II and Cromwell. He himself received a fatal blow to the head with a hammer from a tenant, enraged because he 'paid nobody, and was so ill a landlord and paymaster with so great an estate'. Sir George's cynicism may be understandable. His arranged marriage at age 15 existed in law only, as he and his 13 year-old bride parted on their wedding day. Thus he died without heir, leaving his estate shared between four cousins and the University, with the ensuing conflicts. The site was once far larger, but financial necessity caused a substantial plot to be sold for other University purposes. It remains big enough to serve as Prince Philip's helicopter landing pad when he visits as the University's Chancellor.

Right: *King George III would surely approve of Downing's newest addition: the Maitland Robinson Library, continuing as he originally requested, in a style definitely 'not Gothic'. Its traditional Greek lines and Doric pillars are complemented by the inclusion of its unusual octagonal tower, based on the Tower of Winds.*

Below: *In the old days, the Downing Site was a wetland favoured for hunting waterfowl. As the trees mature, it is becoming a valuable wildlife haven in the heart of the city. Hopefully increasing numbers of wild birds, such as the jay, will re-establish in these verdant spaces.*

Wearing a willow branch is the sign of a successful 'bumping' crew.

ROWING

From a distance, the slender boats glide along the shining water with a grace that suggests effortless elegance. Only when one nears the river bank is it possible to appreciate the awesome surge of power produced by the synchronised efforts of eight determined rowers, directed by their coxswain. The Cam is training ground for the mighty crew that competes each year in the famous Oxford-Cambridge Boat Race along the Thames in London: a tradition begun in 1829.

But there is much more to Cambridge rowing than this celebrated event. Colleges participate in the February 'Lents', and the 'Mays': races held in June during the oddly named 'May Week'. The Cam is too narrow for side by side competition, so in 1827 the system of 'bumping' was devised. The crews are organised into four Divisions, with 16 boats in each. They set off from Baitsbite Lock at one and a half boat length intervals, aiming to bump the boat in front. Bumping may be averted

Preceding page: Trinity Bridge

by 'washing off' the opponent with a wave thrown up by the rudder. The river's course also presents challenges: negotiating Grassy Corner and Ditton Corner has been likened to running round two sharp corners carrying a long ladder. Over four days' competition, boats move up the starting order according to bumping success, with the overall champions becoming 'Head of the River'. Larger colleges can muster more crews, but vociferous support from supporters on the bank, and iron resolve of the team may overcome the toughest odds. Sidney Sussex, with only ten men, managed to come 7th overall one year. Heroic verse recalls the event:

> *'There were eight to row and one to steer,*
> *And one to run on the banks and cheer.'*

Right: Safety measures are essential. Many years ago an unfortunate rower was killed by the sharp prow of a boat which overran while bumping. Boats now have a protective knob affixed to prevent fatalities, but the coxswain is required to acknowledge a bump immediately by raising a hand, and both boats pull over as the rest sweep past.

PUNTING

The experience of punting at Cambridge depends very much on your chosen time of day and which section of the river you prefer. There is no need to exert yourself. Chauffeur punters are ever present around Quayside and Silver Street, and will provide a commentary on your journey, though the tales told could well be embroidered for entertainment's sake! Naturalists might best enjoy a trip from Silver Street to Grantchester early in the morning, when bird life is seen and heard in abundance, and the soft light creates enchanting ripples and reflections on the water. Contemplative historians may prefer the stretch between Quayside and Silver Street early or late in the day, when the ancient tranquillity of the college Backs seems preserved from centuries ago. Either trip will appeal to the Romantic, but a candlelit journey might be the most special of all, particularly if accompanied by a cosy rug and bottle of wine. By contrast, the fun of joining the throng with a group of friends on a sunny afternoon, getting tangled in the willow branches and drifting helplessly sideways into the course of a 'bus punt' full of tourists, could become the happiest of Cambridge memories.

Low bridges require adaptation of method.

Left: Cambridge punts are propelled from the back, unlike their Oxford counterparts, but the basic principle is the same. Let the pole slide through the hands into the water, and lean on it to push the boat forward before twisting the pole free and lifting it out. Care is recommended, as the tales of dislodged punters are no myth!

Left: The Bridge of Sighs

Overleaf: The Mathematical Bridge

Cambridge students celebrate the end of their exams with 'May Week': two weeks of rowing competitions and 'May Balls', held in early June. These lavish parties go on all night, and the 'survivors' often punt up to Grantchester for a very early breakfast at the Orchard Tearooms. This serene journey would be a memorable experience for anyone. For a student released from the frenetic intensity of study associated with examination time, the sense of fun and freedom gliding home from Grantchester on a fine summer morning must reach almost fairytale status.

Dropping down the river,
Down the branchéd river,
Through the hidden outlet
Of some happy stream,
Lifting up the leafy
Curtain that o'erhung it,
Fold on fold of foliage
Not proof against the stars....
Musical the rippling
Of the tardy current,
Musical the murmur
Of the wind-swept trees,
Musical the cadence
Of the friendly voices
Laden with the sweetness
Of the songs of old.

Right: Crusoe's Bridge   James Payn, 1830-1898.
Overleaf: Clare Bridge   From *Poems*, 1853

GRANTCHESTER

The Cambridge experience cannot be truly complete without seeking out the timeless peace of this most English of villages. Its main street and church remain largely unchanged. Even when thronging with visitors its ambient calm remains undisturbed. Situated two and a half miles out of town, it can be reached by punt or along a footpath parallel to the river, known as the 'Grantchester Grind'. Either approach is delightful, with views of the Grantchester Meadows, owned by King's College, and the distant spires of Cambridge behind.

The recently renovated church of St. Mary bears signs of its connections with Corpus Christi college in its pelican and lily decorations. It is noteworthy for its beautiful 14th century chancel, but is most famous for its place in Rupert Brooke's heartfelt poem, 'The Old Vicarage, Grantchester'. Brooke is not the first poet to draw inspiration from this idyllic setting. Tennyson and Chaucer both make reference to the mill, which burnt down in 1928. Byron is said to have loved swimming a little further upstream in the secluded pool, now named after him, and Wordsworth found peace where,

> 'Beside the pleasant Mill of Trompington
> I laughed with Chaucer in the hawthorn shade:
> Heard him, while birds were warbling, tell tales
> Of amorous passion'.

Rupert Brooke's love for the village where he took refuge from the demands of academic life is plain in the poem he wrote while staying in the Café des Westens, Berlin.

> '...laughs the immortal river still
> Under the mill, under the mill?
> Say, is there Beauty yet to find?
> And Certainty? and Quiet kind?
> Deep meadows yet, for to forget
> The lies, the truths, and pain? ... oh! yet
> Stands the church clock at ten to three?
> And is there honey still for tea?'

Left: Wright's Row cottages

In the 1950s, two more poets discovered the joyful release of wandering in the meadows around Grantchester. Ted Hughes, and his future wife Sylvia Plath spent many hours absorbing the tranquillity together. Sylvia recalls in a letter to her mother,

'Got up at 4.30 am this day with Ted and went for a long walk to Grantchester ... I felt a peace and joy in the most beautiful world with animals and birds ... we began mooing at a pasture of cows, and they all looked up, and as if hypnotised, began to follow us in a crowd of about twenty across the pasture to a wooden stile, staring fascinated. I stood on the stile, and in a resonant voice, recited all I knew of Chaucer's Canterbury Tales for about twenty minutes. I never had such an intelligent, fascinated audience'.

The journey to Grantchester may work up a thirst, if not a healthy appetite. There are several pubs in the village, but if you wish to capture the atmosphere which has inspired so many, the Orchard Tearooms may be the best choice. This was a favourite haunt for Brooke and his friends, including philosopher Bertrand Russell, novelist E.M. Forster and Virginia Woolf. Today students traditionally enjoy a very early champagne breakfast here after their May Balls.

Left and opposite: Deckchairs at the Orchard Tea Rooms

The green Pavilion, sheltered beneath ancient apple trees, remains almost as it was at the turn of the century. It is open all year round, but is perhaps most enchanting when the blossom is out, and the vegetation is alive with bird song. Time does seem to stand still in this leafy sanctuary; elevenses can blend effortlessly into lunch time. But it is hard to be energetic after a large meal, so a little rest, watching the birds enjoy any crumbs that may have fallen, seems quite natural. If the sun is hot, you can always pop back for a cool drink. If the sun goes in, an early cup of afternoon tea could be a better choice. It is rare to see so many tempting cakes though: perhaps just one to go with the tea...?

THE AMERICAN CEMETERY

Three thousand eight hundred and eleven members of the American armed forces, who gave their lives in World War II, are represented in this tranquil setting on Madingley Hill. The pure white marble Latin crosses, and Stars of David for Jewish servicemen, stand in arcs radiating out from the pole where the American flag flies. Nothing can prepare the visitor for the emotional effect of this immense and elegant memorial, its immaculate perfection starkly poignant in the light of its brutal and tragic history.

The site, donated by Cambridge University, was dedicated in 1956 as the only American World War II cemetery in the British Isles. Long rectangular pools reflect the chapel and museum at one end, which contains a campaign map engraved by David Kindersley's Cambridge workshop. The Wall of the Missing, that runs the length of the pools, bears the names of 5127 more members of the American forces lost between 1942 and 1945, who 'rest in unknown graves'.

Right: Statues representing the different elements of the United States armed forces keep a silent vigil along the Wall of the Missing. They stand guard over the headstones: a memory of Americans set amongst the peaceful English landscape that they helped to defend.

Overleaf: Evening light over the American Cemetery

THE MAKING OF THIS BOOK

Andrew Pearce has been inspired by the beauty of Cambridge for many years. The college gardens and their wildlife are a special subject, along with the city's changing seasons which give endless variations of light and colour to be captured on camera. His work may also be seen in the Fotogenix range of greetings cards and calendars. Fotogenix Publishing was established to capitalise on his extensive archive of images, accumulated over ten years. 'A Cambridge Keepsake', his third publication, depicts the city's moods throughout the year. This book also aims to capture the human side of the Cambridge story. It has been carefully researched and written by Debi Pearce to provide an insight into the individuals who played a part in its illustrious evolution. We owe many thanks to the archivists and bursars of the colleges, who so kindly advised us. The college websites have also been invaluable. This project could not have gone to print without the assistance of the following: Louise Evans, Steve Pearce, Marianne Pearce, Juliette, Janet, Jeremy McInerny, Penny Fulcher, Catriona Northridge, Laura Webber, Dr. Ruehl, Nicky Boardman, Mary Chapman, Clair Goodhead, Terrie Rogers, Bob Mitchell and Jon Beech.

Left: The architect of the University Library was Sir Giles Gilbert Scott, who also designed the red telephone box, Liverpool Cathedral and Battersea Power Station.

BIBLIOGRAPHY

This College Studded Marsh *Robert Kenny,* **Leaflets of Local Lore** *W.R. Brown* (Newton and Denny), **In Praise of Cambridge** *Sydney Waterlow* (Constable), **Life in Old Cambridge** *M.E. Monckton Jones* (Heffer), **Cambridge Observed: An Anthology** *C. Moseley & C. Wilmer,* **A Walk Through Historical Cambridge** *F.A. Reeve* (Newton & Denny), **Trinity College: An Historical Sketch** *G.M. Trevelyan,* **Cambridge Characters** *Irene Lister,* **Cambridge Commemorated** *Fowler & Fowler* (C.U.P). **Cambridge and its Colleges** *A. Thompson* Methuen, **Cambridge** *J. Steegman* Batsford, **Portrait of Cambridge** *C.R.Benstead* (Robert Hale), **Life in Cambridge** *Louis T. Stanley* (Hutchinson), **Devas & Pearce's Cambridge** *C. Devas* (Midsummer Publishing), **Cambridge Colleges** *J. Jeacock,* **King's College Chapel** *R. Ackerman,* **Cambridge** *M. Hall* (Pevensey Press), **Victorian and Edwardian Cambridge** *F.A. Reeve* (Batsford), **The City of Cambridge Official Guide** *J. & M. Jeacock* (Jarrold), **Cambridge Between Two Wars** *T.E.B. Howarth,* (Collins), **Cambridge** *N. Barnwell* (Blackie & Sons Ltd.), **Cambridge & District** *Ward Lock & Co.* **Introduction to Cambridge** *S.C. Roberts* (C.U.P). **Illustrated Guide to Cambridge** *F. Rutter* (W. Heffer & Sons Ltd.), **Rides Around Cambridge** *E. Conybeare* (W. Heffer & Sons Ltd.), **Cambridge: A Photographic Celebration** *K. Wallis* (Fotogenix Publishing), **Bedders, Bulldogs and Bedells: A Cambridge Glossary** *F. Stubbings* (C.U.P.), **Sidney Sussex College: A Short History** *C.W. Scott-Giles* (Pendragon Press) **Trinity Hall** *C. Crawley* (Printed for the College, Cambridge University Printing House)

Right: Coe Fen in early summer

ADVICE FROM
A CANDID FRIEND, 1673

Do not go to *Cambridge*, Sir, there are *Alehouses*, in which you *will* be drunk. There are *Tennis-Courts*, and *Bowling Greens* that *will* heat you to an excess, and then you *will* drink cold small Beer and die. There is a River, too, in which you *will* be drowned; and you *will* study yourself into a Consumption, or break your *Brain*.

The natural beauty of a rainbow frames the
splendour of King's College Chapel.

Left: The Chancellor's Centre, Wolfson College

INDEX

Right: Whewell's Court, Trinity College

The Judge Institute of Management Studies